Praise for *Great~itude*

"In my 24 years with Goodwill, I have witnessed the transformative power of selfless gifting, as opposed to mere giving, as a steppingstone to self-worth, confidence, and purpose. Through Linda's insightful guidance, you'll transition from isolation to becoming a valued member of a compassionate community, fostering genuine connections with heart-centered individuals and a joy-infused existence."

Toni Giffin
President and CEO
Goodwill Industries of San Diego County

~

"As a Licensed Marriage and Family Therapist in practice for over 30 years I've seen a rise of epic proportion in loneliness. This topic by Linda Lattimore is timely. Loneliness shows up clinically as people of all ages feel disconnected from themselves and others. Without a sense of belonging people feel depressed, anxious, and ultimately devalued. Lattimore's solutions to get into action through service to others are right on. It should be on every counselor's referral list as inspiration for patients who are searching to escape loneliness, elevate self-esteem, and find meaning in life again."

Denise Ross
Marriage and Family Therapist

~

"Employees consistently tell us that isolation is one of the biggest drawbacks of remote working - even though overall they are happy. They miss team lunches, company volunteer programs, and chit-chat at the coffeepot. Since their work connections are confined to phone or video chat, many are looking for one-on-one connections outside of work and home. It's not always easy. If you are an employer interested in the mental wellbeing of your employees, Great-itude offers hundreds of ways for them to connect with others and feel good about their efforts. It's a win-win for both of you!"

Kim Carpenter
CEO/Principal
People at the Center

~

"Loneliness is a signal that an essential need, the desire to belong, isn't being met. Linda Lattimore's book, Great-itude, is a welcome addition for those of us working hard to offer programs that enrich the lives of our seniors, ones that will keep them healthy, engaged, and involved in the world. And, for readers who may feel disconnected in this fast-paced world. It offers easy and doable solutions to this critical issue through small acts of service that enrich the lives of both the giver and the receiver--making them feel valued and an important part of our community."

Simona Valanciute
President and CEO
San Diego Oasis

It takes a village and you are
an important part of ours!
Linda Lattimore

great-itude

OVERCOMING LONELINESS
IN A DISCONNECTED WORLD

LINDA LATTIMORE

SOLUTIONARIES PRESS

First published by

SOLUTIONARIES PRESS

Great-itude: Overcoming Loneliness in a Disconnected World © 2024
by Linda Lattimore

First edition

Paperback ISBN: 978-0-9966117-0-1

Cover art and interior by KH Koehler Design

Printed in the United States of America

To Hayes, Eleanor, Georgia, Walter, and Calvin

The gatekeepers of our future.

Great~itude

Overcoming Loneliness in a Disconnected World

Linda Lattimore

Contents

Acknowledgments

I doubt that I would have turned a daily habit that I was cultivating into a journal and workbook for others without the genuine enthusiasm of my friend Jan Goss, who lit up like a lightbulb (she always has that incandescent glow) when I told her about my evening reflections about my days.

"Oh, that's soooo good! I have a bunch of clients and friends that could really use this book right this very minute—I bet you can write it in four days!" That Texas twang was in full throttle, and being the trout that I am, I was hooked before I even knew that the hook had been set. Nor did I know exactly what I was writing about.

In fact, I didn't fully comprehend that the heartache I felt sometimes was a deep sense of loneliness and disconnection. But, I did understand the concept of give and take, and it was clear to me that every act of kindness is returned in some way and at some point in time—if there is no expectation by the doer of compensation, either monetarily or emotionally. It must be given quietly and free of charge.

I started writing, and as I started to gain clarity, Sandie Marrinucci showed up and began to write with me. She has been my partner in crime in so many writing activities over the years. It was her love and encouragement to help me realize a passion project that helped prime the pump and that kept me committed to writing four to five chapters each week. With me well on my way, she went off to continue her own creative endeavors at Unbridled Communications.

Charles Parisi, another wordsmith and creative genius in the media world (CEO of Cloudcast Media), sat with me over coffee as we noodled over the title, which I had nicknamed *My Value Journal* at the time. I was concerned that someone might think it was about imposing values and judgment when, really, what I wanted was for people to feel more valuable. He loved *Great-itude*, then I loved *Great-itude,* and then you all fell in love with it just as you did with *Solutionaries.* There is just something about newly minted words! It said it all—it's about having a great attitude because of the small, but important, ways we each add value to other people's lives...or our own.

Toni Giffin, the CEO of Goodwill Industries of San Diego County, opened my eyes to populations that I had never considered as interested readers. She believed that this book could be a tool for women housed in safe places—women who have lost all sense of value because they have been told they are worthless. By stepping into a giving role, they might be able to understand their unique contributions and importance, one small step at a time.

Other nonprofit leaders thought it could help disadvantaged teens, the elderly, and those searching for work. The corporate world shared the isolation so many of their employees felt living and working in the remote world of work, some facing company restructurings and leadership changes. I am reminded everywhere I go by everyone I talk to that loneliness is not confined to age, gender, or geography.

To make sure I was high-stepping to the finish line, Felena Hanson (CEO of Hera Hub), a kindred spirit of many years, invited me to a video call about loneliness before the book was in the final publication phase. She quickly followed up with a book teaser to start promoting this work to others. This gave me the gas to get to the finish line in less than a year since that first call with Jan. My thanks also go to K.H. Kohler, a talented editor and designer who guided me through the final steps of the publication process.

My family offers me daily support. Wherever my dreams take me, they cheer me on, allowing me to shine a light on issues that may be bubbling up or are as old as time. Looking at the faces of five small grandchildren, all seven years and under, reminds me that we must pave the way for them to have the support and solid connections they will need to succeed both personally and professionally. Our actions will teach them how to find it on their own.

There are many ways to lose a sense of self, and with each conversation I experience, my faith is renewed that we will find each other again if we will just offer a hand to a friend or a stranger. My heartfelt thanks to each of you for extending yours to me, for making my efforts feel valued, seen, and appreciated—and for removing barriers that keep us from coming back together, brick by brick.

Linda Lattimore

And if it's true we are alone,
we are alone together,
the way blades of grass
are alone, but exist as a field.
Sometimes I feel it,
the green fuse that ignites us,
the wild thrum that unites us,
an inner hum that reminds us
of our shared humanity.
Just as thirty-five trillion
red blood cells join in one body
to become one blood.
Just as one hundred thirty-six thousand
notes make up one symphony.
Alone as we are, our small voices
weave into the one big conversation.
Our actions are essential
to the one infinite story of what it is
to be alive. When we feel alone,
we belong to the grand communion
of those who sometimes feel alone—
we are the dust, the dust that hopes,
a rising of dust, a thrill of dust,
the dust that dances in the light
with all other dust, the dust
that makes the world.

"Belonging" by Rosemerry Wahtola Trommer
All the Honey

Linda Lattimore

Preface

I am the eternal helper bee. It is a trait often found in women who have been raised to multitask as mothers, lovers, business executives, house managers, guides, chauffeurs, chief cooks and bottle washers. I'm told it's an admirable quality, but it's easy to wake up each day feeling depleted as you give shards of yourself away as you try to make others whole. For many of us, this constant need to help and fix is a call to feel important, cherished, needed, and valued.

Every day we put on our superwomen cloaks to mask the lack of appreciation we so often feel from those we serve. We forge breathlessly ahead with our task lists, scrambling to keep the balls in the air and everyone's happiness factor intact. Then we feel guilty because we believe that we are either doing the many roles poorly or we feel resentful as our shield begins to fray at the edges. Our only solution is to work harder and to look for more approval as our emotional tanks begin to drain to a perilously low level.

Men feel alone on this treadmill, too, faced with the social stigma of vulnerability if they share their feelings. They are taught to be tough, brave, and independent, so many remain silent about their needs. A large percentage of men claim they have no close friends or social outlets, focusing exclusively on work and their careers as a means of emotional fulfillment in an effort to take care of their families in the best way they know how.

And then, one day, the race is paused or comes to a dead stop. It shows up as a loss of a job or business, the death or estrangement of a loved one, the vacant house of the empty nester, age, a belief we are invisible, or a global pandemic. We may feel a sense of exile from the world and a lack of value because our value was always tethered to "doing" and seeking appreciation from others.

As a population, we are told by the media, our religious institutions, coaches, and confidantes to be thankful for what we have and not to focus on what we don't have. Gratitude journals sell by the millions, a salve with the sole purpose of teaching us to be grateful for what has been bestowed upon us by the universe, God, or "life." They concentrate exclusively, and with an unbalanced focus, on the concept of being in receipt and being thankful, no matter how unsatisfied we feel.

These journals rarely reflect upon our "other" role in the give and take of good fortune, how there is no blessing without an equal exchange of *energy*. *Note: By energy, I do not mean the physical efforts of constant "doing" in search of remuneration, both financially and emotionally from others.* So, what is the difference? After all, we have been taught that value is a currency based on giving and taking.

The concept of value shows up when we use our financial resources to buy something. It is a fundamental exchange in friendships, love relationships, and partnerships. We receive food, water, and clean air from our planet when we take care of it. And, today, we are more focused than ever on ensuring that this chain is not broken to preserve humanity. There is no limit to value in all of its many forms, and no one kind of value hovers over another. But nothing is free. If you don't give, you don't get.

Like many others, I was incredibly lonely during the onset of the pandemic, stuck in a home isolated without human contact other than two-dimensional video calls. The fear and unknown about this life-threatening illness eventually passed, but, like many, I was left with vestiges of PTSD, having a hard time picking up the pace and returning to the world I had known. I had found my way back to appreciating the basics and to living with less, and I did not have the energy to reconstruct a complicated life—I was short on desire and "mojo."

I felt disconnected from the people and the life I had led. Without the social component, I wasn't experiencing the value exchange that I needed emotionally to feel in sync with the world. My children were grown up, living in different cities with families of their own. I was not getting the "Atta boys" face to face at work or the closeness of friends who were suffering from their own remnants of a confined world. I felt very little forward momentum in my life, and I was working hard to bar the doors to depression. My emotional tank was empty.

One morning, I shared with a friend that I was tired of gratitude journals, and that they weren't making me feel any better. Out of my library of gratitude journals, I had chosen a familiar one and begun writing the same list night after night, short of a few exceptional moments that occasionally appeared. "I'm grateful for my children. I'm grateful I have a roof over my head. I'm grateful for my dog, etc." I skimmed over entries from bygone years and, no surprise...they were the same.

My heart was masked in heaviness as I waited...and waited...to be "bestowed" some sort of miraculous gift that would change both my life and my view of life. I yearned to feel valued and appreciated, to believe that I could make a difference in our world and its inhabitants, which was heavily tilted, wobbling as it figured out how to reboot. The issues were big, and many of us felt paralyzed and unclear as to how to move forward. We were waiting for the universe and others to add value to our lives with vaccines, the fix of supply chain issues, climate change solutions, and the eradication of human rights topics.

Slowly, I woke up to the fact that I couldn't sit around waiting for others to lift my spirits. The cure for my discontent needed to come from within. I was going to have to pat my own back and fill my own reservoir with the personal knowledge that I had made a difference that day. To break old habits and to ensure that I wasn't waiting on reinforcement from others, my mission would be secret, and gratitude for my efforts could only come from one source—me.

I started making a list each night of everything I had done during the day to enhance another person's life or the world at large. Some days, I helped my daughters out with my grandparenting skills. On others, I mentored teens through community service work. I ran free masterminds for women vets who were starting businesses. I was reveling in their success and opened my network to people looking for their dream jobs. There were times I listened to a friend who was struggling with cancer or gave a quarter to a neighbor who needed it for the dryer. Sometimes, it was just a smile for a stranger.

I prayed that I would begin to find myself through my actions, and not my expectations of others. I had my paying clients but, often, that work felt task-centered as opposed to heart-centered. This was stealth, a secret only I knew about. Within weeks, I scratched the word *Gratitude* off the journal and replaced it with *Great-itude* as a reminder that I could feel great by doing great things.

And, here is what happened. Each night, I reflected on my contributions and wrote a list in my journal. The more I added, the more my sense of self-worth was restored as I reminded myself daily that my efforts were important and that the only person who needed to know that...was me. I began to smile a little broader and to engage more freely with others about the work they were doing in the world without feeling left behind. I became watchful and acutely conscious of this value exchange, my senses heightened by the lookout for value in its many forms.

It showed up as lost coins on the sidewalk, perfect parking spots, better relationships, and new and exciting work opportunities. Most importantly, I felt reconnected with the world again. The energy exchange of value was in full swing. I was both giving and receiving from this universal, though invisible, bank account. The greater the deposits, the greater the interest payments. There was a balance and a rhythm to this exchange that I found encouraging and comforting. And, only then did I say thank you because the universe was saying thank you to me.

I have come to believe that there is a collective vault where value in its many forms is stored by those who choose to make a deposit. Sometimes, we add to it and, at other times, we take from it. It's the cycle of life, or like the waves—it moves in and out. This give and take is rarely simultaneous. Rather, it happens in increments over a lifetime. The more we fill this vessel to ensure that it stays full, the more the overflow is returned to us.

I know many people who are feeling off-kilter and out of sorts these days. Whether we are looking for meaningful work in a lackluster job, perceived as too young with a limited skillset and network, tagged as part of a racial or gender minority, or facing age discrimination with hard-earned qualifications that are suddenly expendable because of limited shelf life, each of us yearns for a quality and richness to our lives that may seem elusive.

Here is the good news: You can have it if you are willing to do a little tweaking and modifying of old beliefs that no longer serve you and if you are willing to play the long game, which may not provide an immediate return or quid pro quo. Remember, for the purposes of this exercise, your only goal is to add value to the world around you and to feel good about it, not seek value for yourself. It will show up when you least expect it, multiplied many times over and from many sources.

This journey is designed to help you prime the value exchange pump and feel part of our world again. Each week, you will choose a weekly essay to reflect on and the ways you can participate in enriching someone else's life—or your own. After all, when you are happy, the world around you is happier, too! You can go in the order that they are provided or skip around. The important part is to spend a week on each one and complete all 52 weeks. I promise you that if you are consistent, your life will change in ways that, today, you can't even imagine.

Throughout this 52-week journey of self-discovery, you will:

- Move from powerless and uninspired to being reawakened with a renewed passion for life.

- Go from isolated to visible and an important member of a community of heart-centered people.

- Experience the difference between bargained giving and selfless gifting.

- Feel validated and heard, increasing your feelings of self-worth as your positive impact on the world grows.

- Be recognized for your great attitude (*"great-itude"*) as you begin living with a joyous heart, open and aware of the beauty around you.

I hope you will find this journey as empowering and enlightening as I did. But, most of all, I hope that you will find your way to the home that is you!

Authenticity

One of my favorite childhood books is *The Velveteen Bunny*. It's full of great teaching moments. The most memorable is the core theme about the meaning of "real" explained through the eyes of a little stuffed animal who no longer feels seen by a child. We are reminded that the exterior we present to the world, even when we look worn and frayed, is not what makes us real. Rather, it's our unique and special qualities, ones memorable to others.

Not a day goes by that we aren't reminded to "be true to ourselves" and to be authentic. But, it's not always easy to figure out what our authentic self is if we have become accustomed to conforming to society's expectations. Our values are clear indicators, and if those are fuzzy, too, take a few minutes and reflect on circumstances that have shifted your perception of the world. If you have been lied to, honesty will be something that may be precious to you. If spirituality is a cornerstone in your life, your faith will be your North Star. If you yearn for family, you will seek its comfort in the presence of those who love and support you.

Knowing our values is not enough. Others need to see them through our actions. Most of us have been conditioned to follow the rules or abide by certain cultural mores even when our hearts tell us to go in a different direction. That's when a strong dose of courage comes in, as well as the knowledge that only when we listen to that little voice inside and walk our own path will we be truly happy. People pleasing becomes a thing of the past, and our authentic self appears rather than our adaptive self.

Authenticity is contagious. The more you act like the real you with others, the more those around you will show up being themselves. It inspires loyalty, engagement, and respect because others trust that what we say and do is true. Below are some ways that we can work on becoming our most authentic selves this week:

1. Write a paragraph about your personal brand. Now take a quick survey and ask a small group of friends how they would describe you. Not quite in sync? Remember that you control your brand by your actions.

2. Share a detail about your personal life with a co-worker to help them relate to you. Similar experiences spark conversation and show vulnerability on your part.

3. Offer honest and constructive feedback to a friend, co-worker, or student, and highlight what you believe they did right and how they could do better, then finish the conversation with an encouragement that they are on the right path.

4. Encourage your employees to open communication and foster teamwork by expressing their best and most truthful selves and showing respect for others around them.

5. Give a journal to your teen or grandchild and encourage them to write about their everyday experiences and see how they react and show their true self.

6. Step out of your comfort zone and garner respect by asking three questions this week about things you have always wanted to know but were too uncomfortable to ask. This shows others a genuine curiosity and lack of fear.

7. Post your boundaries in a visible place as a reminder. Have you allowed people to cross them for so long that they have become blurred? What are your negotiables and non-negotiables?

8. Dress in clothing that allows you to display your personality like

you did as a small child. Ditch the fashion trends and find your younger spirit again!

9. Review your circle of influence, those people whom you affect and those that affect you in some way. Do they support your efforts, believe in your dreams, and lack judgment about your truth?

10. Volunteer on a charity project this week. Unlike working for pay, this is heart-centered work where you can take off the mask and set the shield down. It's the perfect time to just be yourself!

Notes:

Creativity

Recently, a friend told me that they didn't have a creative bone in their body, and I challenged them on the statement. Somehow, the word "creativity" often gets translated into "artistry," and they are not the same, although artistry can be a form of creativity. We are all creative in one way or another.

Have you ever solved a problem for yourself or someone else? Of course you have! If you were missing one ingredient for a recipe and substituted another, you were creative. If you helped your child out of a jam at school, you were creative. If you survived a global pandemic, I guarantee you that you were creative—over and over again!

What is creativity and why is it important? It's a quality or skill that allows us to view things with a new perspective, and it reflects our flexibility and tolerance. When we are creative, we study multiple solutions to solve a problem. It's almost always an eye-opening experience, and, often, we discover something new and valuable.

Creativity is not always about problem solving. Often, it's a way of expressing our unique ideas and values. This can be done through many mediums, including art, gardening, writing books, giving speeches, culinary exploration, or innovating new products. Each day we are given a multitude of opportunities to express our true selves and communicate our unique and special thoughts and ideas with others.

Only 25 percent of people believe they are creative. I have a sneaking suspicion that this is because one of the biggest obstacles to creativity is the fear of failure. If we are constantly censoring our thought processes or judging our own efforts, we may find that we are taking the easy way out and simply deem ourselves noncreative.

This is your week to shift that perception and spend a little time reviewing all the ways that you are imaginative each day. When we are creative, we add immense value to the world because it is the lifeblood of progress, both for our individual selves and for the rest of humanity. Below are a few suggestions to get you started.

1. Invite friends to take an evening painting class from a local art studio. Bring drinks and snacks to share and rejoice in their different interpretations of the same subject matter.

2. Take a writing class at your local community college and practice using your imagination to come up with multiple endings to a story.

3. Keep a small journal (an "idea book") with you and jot down ideas the minute they come to you.

4. Pick up a copy of Julia Cameron's book, *The Artist's Way: A Spiritual Path to Higher Creativity,* and find new ways to explore your personal creativity.

5. Have a vision board party and think about what it is you desire in life, what life will look like when your goals and dreams are reached, and how it will feel. Create a collage of this vision and hang it next to your desk.

6. The next time you are faced with making a decision, try the interesting exercise of mind mapping. Explore mind mapping tools such as Miro, Mural, Lucidspark, or Canva.

7. Explore the concept of Feng shui and how your environment affects your energy and state of mind. It may be time to clear out

the old and make way for the new!

8. Start or join a mastermind group and brainstorm weekly about the projects each person is involved with or trying to complete. Help everyone move forward.

9. Start a daily meditation practice to clear your mind of clutter and open it to new possibilities and information. Later, write down new thoughts or revelations as they come to you.

10. Celebrate your failures to encourage yourself to try again and be open to new ideas. Buy something you have wanted for a while, pour a glass of champagne, or get a massage. You made an effort when many never even try!

Notes:

Enthusiasm

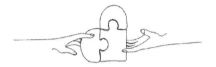

Feeling low on enthusiasm? It can be hard to stay enthusiastic when you are tired, disillusioned, or overwhelmed! But, that's the time to draw strength from within because someone enthusiastic is the master of their own fate. It's better than money, power, or influence because an enthusiastic person is generally persuasive and inspiring to others. Enthusiasm helps you stand apart from those who are critical or judgmental. It can be one of your greatest assets!

When "life gets in the way," I shift my attention to the things that give my life purpose. Enthusiasm is a Greek word that means "inspired by God, a cause, or a movement," so I've discovered that thinking about things that get my juices going are generally the same subjects I read or talk to others about. But, beware, none of us like armchair quarterbacks—those talkers who constantly opine without actively doing anything to help. Action is key. We believe in those that do, not just say they will.

Enthusiasm allows us to focus and helps us prioritize tasks because we generally start checking things off our long "to-do" list by completing the ones that we are drawn to. We feel productive and confident accomplishing a mission that is important to us, believing that we are doing something worthwhile. If our excitement causes others to come along for the ride, we have expanded our positive impact on the world and feel good about it.

This week, check your attitude. It's hard to be inspiring to others if you are convinced that the world and its inhabitants are out to get you! A victim approach kills enthusiasm. And, let's face it, no one wants to be around a Grinch. Instead, take a break, ask for help and support, put a smile on your face, and surround yourself with people who are enthusiastic and positive. Take one small step at a time. Sometimes, you just gotta fake it till you make it!

Enthusiasm doesn't belong to the other guy or gal. It's ours to show our family and friends and anyone else who needs a little encouragement to live their lives to the fullest. Here are some ways to shine your bright light this week:

1. Try using the words *excited, delighted,* or *thrilled* at least 10 times this week in your discussions with others to show passion. Add a smile, and you will find that enthusiasm sparks the same excitement in others.

2. Show your enthusiasm when applying for a new opportunity by explaining exactly what you're willing to do and how far you're willing to go to express your level of commitment. What does "going the extra mile" mean to you?

3. Love to cook and entertain? Create a dinner club with others who have the same passion and alternate homes quarterly for theme dinners. Or discover and support the cool new restaurants in town.

4. Identify the energy suckers in your life, those people that make you feel tired or stressed. Make a conscious plan to spend less time with them and more time with positive people.

5. Find a new hobby or skill that brings you joy and carve out time each week to enjoy a much-needed change to an otherwise monotonous daily routine.

6. Show team spirit at your office by attending holiday functions and enthusiastically participating in team-building exercises. Rally your team to success.

7. Stay on top of the latest innovations by attending conferences, reading publications such as *Fast Co.*, or receiving a weekly newsletter from one of many sources in sectors that interest you such as healthcare, energy, or technology.

8. Be timely with your email responses. While 48 hours may still be considered acceptable, it does not communicate the excitement like a 24-hour turnaround.

9. Look for nonverbal ways to praise or encourage a child. A thumbs up, a smile, or a high-five can be powerful ways to show them you're impressed by their behavior or efforts.

10. Turn drudgery into fun. Think about the things that make a task feel boring and tiresome and what it would take for it to be fun. Then step out of your comfort zone and make it so!

Notes:

Advocacy

Using your voice and expressing your opinion is a precious gift not offered to all, and the views of many people are stifled daily by bullies exercising control through fear. It's hard to watch but it reminds us that advocacy is not in the exclusive hands of lawyers, politicians, and newscasters. It is a privilege given to those who feel free to exercise it.

There are many ways to be an advocate. You can stand up for yourself, champion another, or lobby for a particular cause or policy. I'm sure there are quite a few people you support, including family and friends or those in the public eye who are pushing for reforms you stand behind. You have a deep and genuine belief in who they are and what they can achieve, and when you tell others about their efforts, you are advocating for them.

When we advocate for others or an issue, we must be good representatives, our actions thoughtful and intentional. We do this by staying informed and current, by reading, and researching everything we can about the topics and issues we are drawn to, or enrolling in classes or workshops to learn more about the issues we care about—even the ones that sit at the edge of our comfort zone.

Talking in a non-confrontational way with friends and family who may have differing opinions is a form of advocacy. These conversations give us the opportunity to show curiosity, listen, and express our values and beliefs even as we better understand theirs. Empathy and lack of judgment show our sincerity and openness to growth, a compelling argument to others who might be wavering in their own opinions. In today's conflict-ridden world, this effort to "cross the bridge" of touchy subjects is badly needed.

This week, practice advocacy using your voice for something meaningful to you. Your opinion and brilliance are gifts to the world and add value to many who are unable to express theirs. Focus on the solutions, not just the problems. Most of us will never speak to the media, meet with politicians, or participate in rallies and demonstrations, but there are many other avenues to support the causes and people that you believe in. I've listed some ideas below:

1. Do a little research. Spend your money supporting products, services, and companies that *do* align with your values, and boycott those whose values *don't* align with yours. Consumer spending carries weight!

2. Contact school officials if you learn that a child has been bullied at school or neglected at home. It takes a village to protect our youngest members.

3. Vote in every election. Study the candidates, bills, and platforms, and then make informed decisions. They are your proxy.

4. Speak up for what is best for you. Practice saying "No" if you often take on too many obligations and face burnout regularly.

5. Does a social issue call to you? Get involved with local awareness and fundraising events by participating in walks or fundraisers, speaking at community events, or joining an advisory board of a nonprofit organization.

6. Rehearse or role-play a difficult conversation that a friend expects to have with their boss or teenager.

7. Practice advocacy as a family. Model behavior for your children and grandchildren that shows them it is good to use their voice and stand up for their beliefs and values.

8. It's movie night at your house. Gather family and friends and watch shows about inspirational people who spoke up for others (i.e., *Erin Brockovich, Milk, Selma, The Hate U Give, Hidden Figures*, etc.)

9. Study your local city government's agenda and attend city council meetings. Speak out for action on pressing community issues that you feel strongly about. Be relevant.

10. Offer to be a patient advocate for someone entering the hospital or undergoing a medical procedure. They may need help communicating with healthcare providers to obtain the information they need to make informed decisions.

Notes:

Generosity

I have often thought that being ready to give liberally of your time, money, things, thoughts, or attention without expecting anything in return is one of the most attractive traits we can both experience and bestow on others. In whatever way you give of yourself, each is equally precious and has meaningful value. The key is to do it freely without attachments or expected returns.

Do you consider yourself a generous person? Sometimes, we use the words *giving* and *generosity* interchangeably, but there are a few differences. Are you giving something you were ready to throw away to Goodwill as an easier way to dispose of it? Did you hope to clean out your closets and get a tax write-off with your donation, or were you interested in recycling for the good of the planet and helping another with the purchase of the item at a reduced price? People give every day without being *generous*—an act of pure goodness without any strings attached or benefits expected.

The rewards of being generous often boomerang right back to us. It feels wonderful to receive another's generosity, but the giver also experiences many benefits from these altruistic moments. Generous people are known to have more energy and a sense of gratitude. They are filled with a positive, optimistic outlook that leads to more friends and stronger relationships, all of which are reflected in a greater satisfaction in life, families, and career.

In addition to emotional rewards, there are direct physical rewards to generous people. When you help someone or give a gift, your brain secretes "feel good" chemicals such as Serotonin (which regulates your mood); Dopamine (which gives you a sense of pleasure); and Oxytocin (which creates a sense of connection with others). These benevolent moments directly impact our physical well-being by reducing blood pressure, stress, anxiety, and depression, and by increasing self-esteem.

For a lot of us, it's easier to give than to receive. We deflect compliments, refuse to let friends pick up the occasional lunch tab, or feel awkward asking for help. But, it's helpful to remember that we are creating feel-good moments for others and should show appreciation for their efforts. Give and take is what keeps the balance in our relationships, keeping them healthy and free from the resentfulness that shows up when they are skewed either way.

Our world is hungry for the kindness and generosity of others, and there is a wide array of opportunities for you to experience the special treasures of generosity this week. Below are a few ideas:

1. Use people's names when you talk to them, as well as the words *you* more than *I*. It shows you see them as unique individuals and are listening to what they are telling you.

2. Give someone a homemade gift or something they admire to let them know you remember what they like and that you were thinking of them.

3. Fill a backpack with school supplies for a child in need and include a personal note of encouragement for the first day of school.

4. Be generous with yourself and post positive notes or quotes around your house as a reminder of all of the things that make you special.

5. Help an elderly neighbor figure out local shuttle and bus schedules so they can continue to live independently without driving.

6. Create a social media post about how much you appreciate someone's support or how proud you are of them. Being generous with sincere praise can change the course of someone's day.

7. Teach a free class or workshop at a local community center and share your in-depth knowledge of a topic. Hard-earned wisdom is valuable.

8. Show you are a team player by taking over clean-up duty in a group activity at a volunteer event, work, or school. People will appreciate your efforts.

9. Choose books about generosity for bedtime reading for your children or grandchildren. There are many wonderful examples including *Pass it On, Under the Lemon Moon,* or *The Rainbow Fish,* just to mention a few.

10. Giving away a smile can be a simple, yet impactful, form of generosity. Generosity of spirit can be far more meaningful than financial generosity.

Notes:

Collaboration

Every day we collaborate with people around us, coming together with the hope that we will produce an outcome greater and more successful than anything we can do alone. These efforts take place between friends and coworkers, and strangers and organizations, both near and far. Most recently, we witnessed the work of global scientists who came together in a united effort to save humanity from the deadly effects of the COVID-19 virus. With a common vision of lives over profit, they carried a vaccine to market faster than ever before by sharing research and data.

Collaboration can inspire us and move us from apathy or the status quo to exploring new possibilities with a new and fresh perspective. It's exciting to brainstorm or get feedback on our ideas or pressing issues or to learn from others and share wisdom and valuable insights. It helps us get unstuck and feel hopeful again.

Plus, from a business perspective, there can be cost savings and an extra set of hands to advance various projects you or your organization are moving forward. Teamwork and collaboration boost morale across the organization, and the results are often higher retention rates. It's a great way to integrate new hires into the culture and make them feel that they have a supportive community of co-workers.

Can we be better at collaborating? Yes! It's a skill, so it can be learned. We can practice improving our communication by listening and understanding another person's perspective; taking responsibility for our mistakes; and

43

respecting the diversity of our colleagues. And, we can show we are a team by offering moral support when our partners encounter setbacks or are frustrated with work.

Compromising isn't always easy. It can be stressful and may require a change in mindset. It can be hard to move from complete independence to being part of a team, organizing and delegating tasks, particularly if one partner doesn't pull his weight. However, the benefits of dependability and partnership generally outweigh the challenges if you are committed to seeing things through to the end.

This week make note of ways that you collaborate with others. Here are some ideas:

1. Invite a new friend over and cook a meal together, dividing up the tasks, getting to know each other, and enjoying the fruits of your labor.

2. Exercise once a week with a partner in team sports such as tennis or pickleball, playing to each other's strengths.

3. Join a book club and enjoy the give and take of information about a book you have chosen and read together.

4. Take a comedy improv class and learn how to create a funny moment with a partner or join a troupe and give community performances.

5. Volunteer to be on the board of a nonprofit organization and come together with other leaders in a common vision to help the organization succeed.

6. Join a conversational French or Spanish (or any other language) meetup group where you have coffee and practice speaking a foreign language with another.

7. Become a conflict mediator and help individuals and groups bridge their differences.

8. Invite friends over for game night (i.e., Bunco, Bridge, Mahjong, or Trivial Pursuit). Split the group up into teams and award fun prizes at the end of the evening.

9. Celebrate an achieved goal if you have worked hard with a partner or a team on a particular task...pop the bubbly or go out for ice cream. Alternately, have a team celebration day by playing a round of golf or sailing.

10. Grab some friends and complete an Escape Room challenge. Figuring out how to get out together is a perfect way to bond and have fun.

Notes:

Courage

I have come to learn that having courage is not the *absence* of fear but a triumph *over* fear. Even the most courageous people are afraid. They've simply found something that matters more to them than the overwhelming feeling of terror.

As a single mother for many years navigating financial difficulties and feeling isolated and overwhelmed as jobs came and went, the only thing that mattered to me was the health and welfare of my children. Looking at their sweet faces, nighttime fears would disappear as I made bold asks to keep us moving forward. I soon learned that as terrifying as audacity can be, "If you don't ask, you don't get." This knowledge has opened many doors for me both in personal matters and in my career.

Bravery and finding courage look different for everybody. For the young, fear of what lies ahead may hamper their actions. For the elderly, fear that past mistakes may repeat can create false boundaries or a sense of risk that limits their full enjoyment of life. This lack of comfort and confidence has been known to cause unrest and anxiety, sweaty palms, heart palpitations, or sleepless nights full of fretting about the path forward. Ultimately, it's taking a decision—any decision—that finally calms our minds.

There have been a handful of times in my life when I have been asked in wonder, "How did you make it through? Weren't you terrified?" In reality, I woke up each morning and took one small step, a breath, and then another small and uncertain step forward, often with no destination in sight. I tried hard not to worry about every potential outcome of each questionable situation that was staring at me from the periphery. Eventually, I would make my way through the muck, leaving much of the trauma or disarray in my rear-view mirror.

When was the last time you flexed your courage muscle? Being courageous can be habit-forming if you hone this quality. Your efforts don't have to be groundbreaking; small, regular acts that support your values count! Many wonderful things come from showing courage in addition to feeling empowered and proud. Others will find you inspirational and will start to dig deep and follow suit. Your impact will have a ripple effect.

Here are some ideas. I hope you find this exercise exhilarating!

1. Get comfortable with being uncomfortable. Write down five of your biggest fears and then three steps under each that will help you overcome them. (I.e. if you are afraid of public speaking, join Toastmasters or a theater class.)

2. Take a stance with a colleague who may need support as they make their own tough decisions that they are concerned may be unpopular.

3. Show your vulnerability by asking someone for help without worrying that you might look inept.

4. Stick up for someone who may be picked on, harassed, or bullied even if it puts you "in their camp."

5. Find a mentor who will help you sort through tough decisions and encourage you to walk forward confidently.

6. Give a pep talk to a young person who may feel peer pressure or be afraid to ask another to a first dance or out on a date.

7. Use positive self-talk by posting affirmations around your home or office to give you confidence in your decisions and their outcomes.

8. Join a service group that mentors teens, giving them the self-assurance to embrace failure and seek new skills through higher education or trade school.

9. Try something that may seem a little risky such as ballroom dancing, riding on a motorcycle, rock climbing, or vacationing alone.

10. Delegate work and let someone do something they have never tried before even if you know it could reflect on you as a leader.

Notes:

Forgiveness

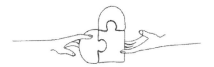

Many of us have experienced betrayal that has brought us to our knees, those times in our lives when we thought all was lost, including the ability to trust. When the person who caused the hurt moves on seemingly without a care in the world, it's confusing, and we can carry that bag of pain around for a long time. We allow ourselves to suffer over and over, and every time we wonder about what caused this wound.

It may be hard to envision a way to rebuild and move forward, especially when the hurt is fresh, emotionally charged, and up front and center in your life. Yet, when we look back at other pivotal points in our lives, we see that, somehow, despite the trials and tribulations, we are in a better place, that we learned and grew. I know that when my heart has been cracked wide open by another, and when I have been at my most vulnerable, light has always shown through the crevices to help me heal and become wiser.

Often, we can't go through this process alone; we need the assistance of professionals to help us process our feelings around forgiveness. Thankfully, there are many resources open to us. These trained and caring people offer a different vantage point than ours in our efforts to achieve the peace of mind we each need and want.

Forgiveness is something we do for ourselves to heal. If we can find a way to be compassionate with others who have hurt us, whether we choose to continue our relationship with them or not, there is a chance we will find a lightness and clarity of mind and purpose that may have been put on hold.

We have nothing to lose and everything to gain.

Here are a few suggestions as we think about the health of our relationships this week:

1. Journal about what needs to be healed in your life—who you need to forgive and why. List a few ways to begin. One might be to write a forgiveness letter to someone to begin your healing process.

2. Build your compassion and empathy for others by listening to their stories. Imagine what it would be like to walk in their shoes and how you would feel.

3. Join a support group or see a counselor to help you move past the pain.

4. Learn to accept the flaws and imperfections of others and think about why they trigger you. Could it be something you are also dealing with? Have you been forgiven by others for those same qualities? How did it make you feel?

5. Read as many stories as you can about examples of forgiveness. Many will inspire you to see that some of the things we carry are petty and insignificant.

6. Step into the shoes of the person who needs forgiveness and write a letter from them to you explaining their side and their remorse. Then write one back owning your role and accountability in the situation. Read both letters out loud.

7. Make a list of the "mistakes" you have made during your life and how, in hindsight, they were learning experiences. Consider the benefits and wisdom you received and how they are applicable today.

8. Do you have moments of thinking you are less than what others see in you, what some call "Imposter Syndrome?" Consider

taking a class to enhance the qualifications you believe you are lacking—i.e., leadership, communication, parenting, etc.

9. Practice mindfulness through meditation and/or yoga to live in a more expansive and detached view.

10. Surround yourself with positive, uplifting people who will set an example and help you let go of the pain and move forward with optimism and confidence.

Notes:

Education

When people exchange ideas, knowledge, and best practices they receive the information they need to make better decisions for themselves and others who might need help. They are introduced to culture, art, and technology, and they gain newfound clarity about the world around them. Often, walls, borders, and lines drawn in the sand shift or crumble with new awareness, and community is built, moving us toward a safer and more harmonious world.

In a power-driven world of "have and have nots," education levels the playing field and provides greater self-dependency and financial stability. It is one of the biggest value makers in our society. Whether you are sharing knowledge with someone else or learning something new yourself, increasing the collective's knowledge gives all of us a sense of purpose and a desire to innovate and create new ideas and concepts.

Education and self-esteem grow exponentially together. Our parents were right. People who are educated are offered more job opportunities. The old adage "practice makes perfect" holds true whether you are learning a new musical instrument or language or the skills to be an excellent speaker. As we grow, so does our confidence and belief that we can accomplish the next step, followed by the next.

I believe that informal education, sometimes known as "street smarts" and "life lessons" is as important as the formal education we receive from teaching institutions. This skill set, learned experientially, allows you to regulate your emotions, and read situations and people. It gives you the tools to manage relationships and communicate effectively. A combination of both is critical to our success!

Nelson Mandela once said, "Education is the most powerful weapon which you can use to change the world," and a day rarely goes by that we don't learn something new, even surprising, that shifts our perception of the world. How are you helping to add wisdom to your life and others? Below are some ideas:

1. Become a cultural mentor to foreign students by teaching English as a second language either locally, online, or on an adventure abroad.

2. Get involved in a cause such as raising educators' pay, school funding, or improving teachers' work environments. Check out the National Education Association for ways you can help.

3. Run a school supply drive for children without financial means. Not quite sure where to begin? There are *many* resources online or find one in your local community and participate at a grassroots level.

4. If you love history, consider training to be a docent at a local museum. Pick out a museum that interests you and request information on their programs. Then take a tour and ask working docents about their experience to determine if it is a good fit for you.

5. Share your passions or talents with teens exploring summer job opportunities. Contact a handful of people within your network and ask them if they will consider hiring a young person for the summer.

6. Volunteer at a senior's community center if you are adept at technology, which changes fast and furiously. Help members stay abreast of the latest trends, assist with buying new equipment, and help them learn new software programs.

7. Host a foreign exchange student for a semester and both share your culture and learn about their own. This is a great way to rediscover local attractions, connect with other people in your community, and add variety to your daily routine.

8. Literacy means access to opportunities for life and a pathway out of poverty for many. Participate in a reading program for children and adults through your local library. Twenty-one percent of adults in America can't read, and you can help change their lives.

9. Sponsor the education of a child through a nonprofit organization. With a little research, you will discover many opportunities. Two that you can check out are World Vision and Save the Children, but there are many opportunities right in your own neighborhood.

10. Everyone studies history in school, but it's travel that brings history to life. It shows us the world as it is today and teaches us about social, political, and economic complexities. Start planning a family trip and learn!

Notes:

Trust

Everywhere we turn, we trust. It's unavoidable. From something as simple as purchasing food from the grocery store or having a nice meal at our favorite restaurant to dropping our children off at school or the surgical team that is performing an open-heart procedure, we are forced to give in to trust.

When we trust, we rely on another person because we feel safe with them and have confidence that they will not hurt or violate us. It is a feeling that allows us to be open to the person without the need to feel protective. There are many ways to both exhibit trust and create trust in another person. Like any other feeling, it can grow or diminish depending on the circumstances.

If we want to have a trusting personal relationship or a trusting work environment, we must do the work to keep trust alive and strong. One way to do that is to take 100 percent responsibility for our lives and our interactions with others without making excuses. This shows that we are honest and transparent and, sometimes, it includes a heartfelt apology which reflects our character and integrity.

Showing empathy for another person's circumstances and needs lets them know we are trying to look at each situation from their perspective. This allows them to feel heard without repercussion even when they are expressing anger and hurt feelings. Our ability to be open and find ways to bring calm to another is a huge boost and helps reinforce trust. It shows people that we care and are trying to be helpful.

There is never a better time than today to examine our trustworthiness and that of the people we associate with. You will have many opportunities this week to practice, but here are a few ways to kickstart your efforts:

1. Take a risk with a friend or partner by signing up for a class together or opening up emotionally. This creates a bond as you learn to trust each other and show your vulnerability on the journey.

2. Make a list of five ways that you could show more respect. Sometimes familiarity breeds contempt. We may not realize that we aren't coming from a place of respect. It's pretty hard to trust someone that you don't respect.

3. Take a communication class and learn ways to present yourself in a way that breeds trust—i.e., look directly into another's eyes during conversation, practice active listening, etc.

4. Can you think of something you have promised another you would do that hasn't been finished? Reliance is a huge component of trust as you look to complete it.

5. Do some journaling today and write down ways that you have learned from your failures or mistakes, and how those lessons may support a challenge faced by another. Did these experiences help you build faith and learn to trust in the process and in universal timing?

6. Encourage and support a spouse with their passion project even if you don't get it. Trust that it is for their greater good that they accomplish it and that they are following their heart. Give a gift of encouragement that relates directly to their new hobby (i.e., paintbrush).

7. Start showing your children that you trust them by giving them responsibilities that may be a little out of your comfort zone.

Watch carefully to see how they manage, and then praise them for their success.

8. Practice fairness with others in both your personal relationships and at the office. Teach this concept to those you mentor, opening the door to more empathy and the idea that everyone at the table can "win" without someone else losing.

9. Submit high-quality work, improve a process, and become an expert. Become the "go-to" person whose words and actions can be trusted to be consistent and accurate, but also be generous with credit where credit is due.

10. Trust is generally built slowly after repeated interactions and can be stripped away quickly. Write a list of ways that you can build a relationship of trust with a new friend or rehabilitate an older friendship.

Notes:

Stress

Our world is experiencing more stress than ever before, and it continues to rise at an alarming rate. Stress levels vary from person to person. Situations that don't bother someone else might cause you a lot of anxiety because people have unique life challenges and individual coping skills. We may find ourselves triggered emotionally by another person, by a lack of sleep, a fear of the unknown, or failure.

Not all stress is in response to adverse situations, it can show up even when there are positive changes like a new arrival, an impending wedding, an exciting new job, remodeling, or moving to a new home.

We often think of the stress response as detrimental, showing up as an elevated heart rate, shortness of breath, or a general sense of despondency. But, in many cases, stress hormones actually induce growth and release chemicals into the body that can rebuild cells and enhance immunity, leaving the body even stronger and healthier than it was before. It builds emotional resilience, which leads to more contentment, inspiration, motivation, and flow.

It's important to know how to separate the things that drain us from the things that energize us. This includes the people around us who leave an impact on us. Secondhand stress is very real because we are sensitive creatures. We can "catch" negativity from others in our highly connected world. We are, after all, hyper-exposed to all forms of media all day long. In return, we can affect the physical and emotional health of others by projecting our own anxiety onto them.

How do we create an emotional barrier to stressors? We can start by paying attention to where worry shows up in our bodies and when it dissipates, writing down our triggers and how they were resolved. Remember, the value that we bring to the world and those in our circle of influence should be uplifting, not diminished by our feelings of anxiety. Below are a few things to consider:

1. Work smarter, not harder, and avoid procrastination. Write down and organize your many tasks and pick three tasks you will commit to finish the next day. The next morning, turn your email and phone off and get these micro-tasks done!

2. One of our many stressors is job hunting. Actively assist someone who is looking for work by introducing them to your contacts, reviewing their resume, or helping them to practice interview skills.

3. Leave the smartphone behind and go for a walk in the sunshine. Or, listen to a captivating audiobook, podcast, or a walking meditation to empty your mind of all the chatter and give it a reprieve.

4. Take someone for coffee who is struggling because of a loss of work, the death of a loved one, illness, or a divorce. Give them your undivided attention.

5. Shop on the perimeter of the store. Fill your cart with ingredients considered brain food such as salmon, blueberries, beets, or avocado. Avoid depressants like processed meats, refined cereals, high-fat dairy products, or alcohol.

6. Get those endorphins up! Discover a new form of physical activity, schedule a yoga class, and learn new breathing techniques to help with anxiety.

7. Work at an animal shelter or snuggle with your own pet. Studies

show that playing with your pup increases your "happy" hormones, and petting them decreases anxiety. It's a win-win for both of you!

8. Learn about Feng shui, the ancient art of arranging buildings, objects, and space in an environment to achieve harmony and balance. Then, make your office or home feel like a creative sanctuary!

9. Manage your social media time with a cap of 30-40 minutes per day. Work can be tedious, and it's easy to become derailed and start scrolling through your Instagram account. But, too often, the news is distressing and not a break at all.

10. Find ways to take the focus off yourself and your own perceived problems and turn your attention outward. Being in service to others creates moments of feeling appreciated and valued. Pain and stress are inevitable, but suffering is optional.

Notes:

Curiosity

If you have children or grandchildren, you probably answer the question "But why?" over and over until you have come to the end of either your patience or your knowledge about the topic. Starting their lives with blank slates, young ones spend their days in constant exploration of the way things taste, feel, and work.

Being curious is important, not just for children but for all of us. It helps us to learn and grow with an open mind, giving us the tools to solve the many problems and issues that face us each day. We are more creative and engaged with the world around us when we come from a place of wonder. In essence, curiosity is what drives our desire to make the unknown known. All great achievements begin with a spark of curiosity.

Often, as we age, we lose a little of that curiosity for life. Our slate is full, our minds overflowing. We may not ask as many questions or take the time to dig deeper into topics that might be interesting as we pivot from one task to another. Although some people are naturally curious, others need to cultivate the art of being inquisitive. In either case, it's helpful to remember that curiosity is an exercise for the mind, another tool to stay sharp and engage with the world.

We all experience curiosity in different ways. Are you an intuitive discoverer, curious about our human experience, hoping to understand the world that we live in? Are you inquisitive about how and why things work, attempting to find better solutions? Do you find it thrilling to seek out and uncover new things through experiments and participation? Or, perhaps, you are an investigator researching the systems that form our world and the universe. The differences are subtle but distinct.

This week, take some time to engage your curiosity and take note of how you feel at those times—whether you feel more connected to life and the people around you or find yourself prompted to try new ways to solve daily problems. Here are a few ways to spark your curiosity:

1. Curious about Thai food, oysters, or different kinds of wines? Ask a friend to join you for dinner to try a new cuisine or wine pairing.

2. Explore a new hobby. Whether it's woodworking, baking, or bird watching, there are many classes available both online and in person. Get creative!

3. Check out Babbel and Rosetta Stone and learn a language that you have always wanted to speak. Practice your newfound skills in the silence of your car on the way to work or at the supermarket!

4. Make it a habit to ask "Why?", "How?", "When?", or "What?" questions this week in all of your conversations. Go deeper—everyone has an interesting story!

5. Finish your college degree or take a certification program in a new field that interests you or one that will help you advance in your career at an accredited online university.

6. Pick up a crossword puzzle before you go to bed, play Wordle or Scrabble on your phone, or invite a group over to play Trivial Pursuit. Practice remembering and learning new words.

7. Discover your heritage through research or cultural exchange programs. Ask a friend to tell you about their ancestors over coffee and then tell them stories about yours. Can you find commonalities?

8. Go on a hike and take pictures of the local scenery and plants. Find out more about them by using apps such as PlantNet, including whether they are dangerous for your pets or will cause a rash, etc.

9. Retool. It's time to catch up with the world of technology. It's moving at warp speed and you don't want to fall behind. Often older generations are accused of being tech-illiterate—time to prove the naysayers wrong!

10. Figure out how things work. Take something mechanical apart with your child or grandchild and see if you can put it back together. Alternately, let them help you build a piece of IKEA furniture following the steps in the guide.

Notes:

Military Families

Unless you have friends or family serving our nation in the military, chances are you may not give them much thought on a day-to-day basis and are probably unacquainted with the many sacrifices they make even though our way of life depends heavily on their bravery and willingness to serve. These devoted citizens work around the clock to protect our nation and each of us.

Military service can mean months or years spent away from loved ones, deployment in a foreign country or at sea, and the willingness to put one's very life on the line to serve our country. In addition, the day-to-day challenges of frequent relocation and family upheaval also affect the trailing spouse's ability to find a job and the average military child will attend between six and nine schools in grades K to 12. There are higher rates of mental health challenges in the children who lack school and friendship stability and who face the reality that a parent may or may not come home from deployment.

Our service members received only a 2.7 percent pay raise for 2022, which pales amid surging inflation rates of over eight percent, forcing as many as 24 percent of military families into food insecurity in the face of what is effectively a five percent pay cut. Though there are some incentives when shopping on the base, the quality and selection are often limited. Some military families report feeling embarrassed that they need to apply for nutritional assistance programs and charitable food aid, and there can be personal repercussions if the military leader's perception is that the service member can't properly manage their money.

There are many ways to support members of our military and their families in their daily lives. Something as simple as thanking a service member for their commitment or acknowledging the immense challenges of life as a military spouse can have a real, positive impact on the military community. Here are a few ways you can offer your support in the coming week:

1. Team up with your child or grandchild and write a letter of thanks or send a care package to a military family (those currently in the service or a veteran) through Operation Appreciation or Operation Gratitude.

2. Provide a temporary home for the pet of a deployed service member. Check out Dogs on Deployment and give someone a sense of relief that their pet is in good hands while they are away.

3. Hire a trailing spouse (or working-age child) or pass along their resume and vouch for them to a hiring manager. Check out Hiring Our Heroes (U.S. Chamber of Commerce Foundation) or the Spouse Ambassador Network (Dept. of Defense) for a list of organizations involved in this initiative.

4. Donate to one of Operation Homefront's many wonderful programs, which include providing rent-free transitional housing and family counseling support when a member of the military has been injured or wounded and is separating from the military and entering the civil sector.

5. Donate gently used wedding dresses to Brides Across America or formal wear to your local USO. They often have clothing programs to ease financial burdens.

6. Use your social media networks to support the online business of a military spouse or make a purchase of their service or product.

7. Find ways to encourage the school community to welcome and include military families. Many schools offer new Family Liaisons

with seats on the PTA/PTO boards. Their goal is to assimilate military children quickly into the campus to make their educational experience a positive one.

8. Invite a military family over for a holiday meal or celebration. Consider donating food or funds to local food banks with programs for military members.

9. If you are a tech professional or a business coach, help NPower, a national workforce nonprofit organization, with free IT training, professional development, job placement assistance, and social support, either virtually or in person, to military veterans and spouses seeking work in the civil sector.

10. Volunteer with military-family organizations like Blue Star Families or the USO. Contact the Family Resource Center at a local base for volunteer opportunities. There are many ways to uplift these families.

Notes:

Surprise

When was the last time someone surprised you with an unexpected fun and thoughtful gesture? The fact that you still remember this act of kindness demonstrates its impact. Surprise, it turns out, helps us live life with more engagement, wonder, and joy.

A good surprise releases feel-good chemicals into the brain. It can be the result of a hug from a friend, the smell of cookies baking, or an unexpected job raise. It not only improves our mood but also increases our tolerance for uncertainty, which can help reduce our anxiety levels.

Sadly, surprises aren't always happy ones. The sudden death of someone you love, the end of a relationship, a weather-related catastrophe, or an unexpected illness are just a few examples of life's harsher surprises—those that may cause us to yearn for predictability and a sense of normalcy. We will all experience both ends of the surprise spectrum at one time or another.

Creating small, spontaneous acts of joy and supporting each other through the dark times is how we overcome hardship and build courage and resilience. A surprise can transform not only the recipient's mood and outlook but yours as well. It's not the value of the gesture but the fact that you cared enough to carry out a spontaneous act of kindness that's important.

People are designed to crave the unexpected—the things that take them out of boredom and return them to the concept of novelty. Consider taking a minute today to surprise someone in your corner of the world. Not only will you unexpectedly lighten up their life, but you'll feel pleased that you made a positive difference. Here are a few ideas to think about:

1. Send a handwritten letter to a friend or relative and let them know how much you appreciate them—not a thank you note for something they did for you but "just because."

2. Collect new journals or inspirational books for prison inmates to show them that someone believes in their rehabilitation. Write a note of encouragement on the first page.

3. Buy a restaurant gift card and ask the waitress to give it to an elderly couple or young family with children after you have left. No thank you is needed, just the knowledge that you did something special for a stranger.

4. Register a star for someone special at one of the online registries. They will receive a special certificate showing them the coordinates, the constellation, and the knowledge that you believe they shine brightly.

5. Print and frame a photo of you with a friend on that unforgettable trip. Or, better yet, create a photo album as a reminder of the special gift of your friendship.

6. Buy tickets to your loved one's favorite event, a baseball game, or a musical. Tuck them away in their nightly reading material with a cute invitation note.

7. Make it a daily habit to send someone a funny e-card who could use a laugh on a chaotic or boring day. Do your best to make it personal to their circumstances.

8. Bring a smile to a loved one's face and do a chore without being asked. Fill the gas tank, vacuum and dust, change the sheets on the bed, and leave chocolates on the pillow.

9. Hang some spring flowers on your neighbor's door or send a plant to the office of someone working long hours. Bring a little nature and sunlight into their space.

10. Adopt a less fortunate family during the holidays, filling stockings for the children with items they not only need but secretly might hope for. Complete the day with a festive meal— enough to have leftovers for a couple of days.

Notes:

Attitude

My father was a deeply devout man with high standards, and I have found myself striving to live up to his expectations my entire life. After he passed, it took a concentrated effort on my part to release that sense of failure when I didn't meet what I perceived to be his level of excellence. I've worked diligently to change my attitude, and my level of anxiety, to one of celebration for my accomplishments. I finally understand that the only person I am responsible for pleasing is the one in the mirror.

Attitude is the way you look at life, your disposition towards others, and the world we live in. Although your attitude can reflect the type of day you are having, it often stems from underlying values and beliefs. Breaking bad habits is hard, particularly if we have adopted our parent's habits that may not ultimately serve us. That certainly was the case for me.

Fortunately, you get to choose your attitude. It is not something that just happens to you; it's created by your thoughts. But, you must have the desire to change your outlook. Sometimes, that desire is hard to find because you are deep in the weeds. It may require a "fake it till you make it" mentality, going through the actions one step at a time until the shift occurs.

One sneak attack I use is to put uplifting and up-tempo music on. I place the alarm across the room with Latin salsa as my morning drill sergeant. I'm forced to get out of bed and walk across the room to turn it off. Inevitably, I find myself smiling and moving to the music, and the tone of my day has shifted before it was set. The truth is, I don't want to wake up feeling sad;

it's not a good feeling.

Take time this week to pay attention to your attitude, both when you are alone and when you are around others. Be aware and check in with yourself throughout the day. Do you inspire others when you are around them, or do you leave them feeling anxious and tired? Do you spend the conversation complaining or talking about others? Do you smile often and receive them in return? These are all symptoms of your attitude.

I've given you some ways below to change your focus this week, but I'm confident you will have many opportunities with your eyes wide open. A happier you is contagious—in a good way!

1. Find your laughter by watching funny movies, going to comedy clubs, or sharing knock-knock jokes with the tiniest members of your family.

2. Vow not to complain for at least 30 days, and put a dollar in the "Complaint Jar" each time you do. At the end of the month, donate the funds to a worthy cause.

3. Clean out your bedroom closets and kitchen cabinets. Donate surplus goods that no longer serve you to organizations aiding others.

4. Start your morning strong by meditating for 10 minutes, playing uplifting music, or reading an inspiring passage. Stay away from the onslaught of bad news in the media until you are fortified with positive thoughts.

5. Ditch the gossip/negative speak with friends who thrive on it and limit your interactions to positive people and environments. Watch out for your own pessimistic thoughts. Do you discourage friends or offer them reassurance?

6. Take a break and breathe. Look around and say thank you for the first thing you see that you are grateful for. Make it a habit to do this at the top of the hour throughout your day.

7. Create beautiful affirmations on Canva or as a fun art project to change your perspective from pain, sadness, or fear to hope, faith, and confidence.

8. Take a dance class and enjoy the camaraderie and music as you improve your cha-cha or two-step.

9. Show your smile throughout the day. Be optimistic, hopeful, and encouraging even if you feel down. You may change another person's attitude.

10. Keep a file of all of the complimentary notes, emails, or referrals from friends and co-workers. Sometimes, we just need a reminder of how great we really are!

Notes:

Caregiving

The human desire to ensure the welfare of others is primal and starts early on when a child rocks her baby doll or plays joyfully with a puppy. As parents, we are tasked with teaching our children how to be more caring individuals. We hope they will learn to be considerate, patient, understanding, and loving.

Sometimes, however, in our desire to model empathy and care, we find ourselves spread thin. The burden of too much caregiving can creep up on us as we take on more and more duties as parents, spouses, grown children, volunteers, and friends. What may start as one favor or helpful task multiplies into many and, quickly, we find ourselves out of balance.

Caregiving is especially hard when it's triggered by a major health event of a loved one. In these situations, it's easy to ignore our own health and mental well-being because we feel guilty if we don't devote a large percentage of our time and emotions to the person in need. Before we know it, caregiving has become our new career, our new normal.

If this is your reality, parenting both young and old because of an urgent situation, you must also nurture your own needs and seek help. How many times have we heard a flight attendant remind us to put on our mask first before our child in case of an emergency? If our well is empty, we have nothing to give.

You may be witness to someone else in the throes of navigating these challenges, I'm sure they could use a little, or a lot, of your wisdom and time because it's a scary season. Below are some ideas to think about for both you and them:

1. Help a friend who is in the throes of caring for an elderly parent by offering to arrange and drive their loved one to and from medical appointments so they can have a small break from their daily routine.

2. Worrying about finances can be debilitating if you are a caregiver, but knowledge is power! There are many resources available. Call your local agency on aging, research funding for caregivers provided by the Older Americans Act, or review Veterans benefits.

3. It can be hard to ask for help. Most of us say we are okay when we might not be. Consider giving a friend a checklist of ways that you can help and ask them to pick one this week. It's a start to the flow of care to the caregiver.

4. Do grocery shopping or set up a meal train for a working parent who finds themselves in the "sandwich generation" caring for children and parents. Even the delivery of one meal a week will be appreciated!

5. If you find yourself overwhelmed with caring for others, remember to carve out time for your mental health. Go for a walk, attend an exercise class, go to the library to read, or have tea with a friend. Your support system is bigger than you think, and they want to help—let them!

6. Listen to the parents of children with disabilities and don't give unsolicited advice. Disabilities are unique and different for every child. Rather, get to know their child personally and spend time with them, giving their caregivers a small break from being on high alert 24/7.

7. Not everyone can afford full-time assistance. Volunteer at Meals

on Wheels, an organization supporting the independence of seniors living alone. Deliver a meal and provide social interaction for those who are homebound and isolated.

8. Spend time with children whose parents are in a demanding caregiving role with a family member. There is a good chance they could use attention and a fun activity solely focused on them or help them with homework and transportation.

9. Volunteer at a caregiver fair or training at your local community center, YMCA, or church, and ask all of your friends to promote it.

10. When intense caregiving has come to an end, often a loved one has passed on. Stress and exhaustion have moved into grief, sadness, and loneliness. Add important annual recurring dates and other memorable information to your contact list and reach out with a call or card.

Notes:

Eco Friendliness

Every day we read about extreme weather events such as heatwaves, droughts, floods, and wildfires, and the effects they have on families. If we are lucky, they have not touched us directly, but they still show up in increased insurance premiums, rising energy and travel costs, and inflated food or product prices.

Earth provides every resource for sustaining both living things and inanimate objects. It gives us food, water, and shelter, which allows us to co-exist in an ecosystem with many plants and animals. It is the only planet that we know of today where life is sustainable, and yet we are systematically destroying our own home through our actions or inaction. One million species could vanish by 2050, and our Earth can only continue to provide for us if we protect its biodiversity.

Many have yet to take steps to minimize the damage they are doing, often because of a lack of education or resources—or sadly, due to apathy. It's never too late to start. Do you consider yourself environmentally friendly, and do you show it with your actions? Are you an educator raising public awareness and teaching your family about options that will help? Has your place of business taken important steps to conserve our resources?

We are all interconnected, and every life form, no matter how small, is essential to the whole. Doing a reset and restoring these ecosystems will help to end poverty, combat climate change, and ensure our children and descendants have a healthy environment and quality of life to grow up in.

Like many, I'm concerned that unless each of us participates in the resolution of the problems that are threatening us, our very existence as a human race will be in peril. But, I have great faith that we will come together and use our brilliance to make our world an even greater place to live, and that we will each take responsibility and fix the damage we have caused. Here are just a few ways that you can participate this week and, in the years ahead:

1. Buy locally produced organic foods and avoid buying foods that must be trucked in from great distances. Study farming practices harmful to the earth and your body and shun foods grown using dangerous chemicals.

2. Invest your money through social impact funds in environmentally and socially conscious publicly traded businesses that care about their effects on the world around them. Or, support a startup whose mission to provide innovative products or services resonates with your desire to leave a positive imprint on our world.

3. Maintain and tune up your vehicle regularly for maximum gas mileage. Consider and research new electric vehicles as an option for your next purchase.

4. Don't buy aerosols, Halon fire extinguishers, or other products containing CFCs that are harmful to both you and the atmosphere.

5. Introduce your family and friends to your favorite eco-friendly products and services and raise awareness. Many newsletters and websites filter and present interesting new products.

6. Volunteer to do something "pro-Earth" with other kindred spirits. Organizations are always looking for reliable and committed people to assist them with events, fundraisers, and even yard work.

7. Don't buy new every time and set up swaps with friends so

unwanted items stay out of the landfill and older items are given a new lease on life. Consider checking out items from your local library. Many are no longer limited to books and media.

8.   Donate to a clean water charity or any other movement that calls to you that helps our planet. Support others who are the "boots on the ground."

9.   Swap out meat and dairy items for plant-based options. Eighty percent of all greenhouse gas emissions are associated with livestock production.

10. Cut your use of single-use plastics and paper by 50-75 percent. It takes 450 years for it to decompose, so make sure that yours is recycled multiple times.

Notes:

Beauty

Close your eyes for a minute and think about the last beautiful thing you saw or heard. Was it the smile on your beloved's face when you opened your eyes this morning? The sound of children laughing and playing outside your window? The sun sinking slowly into the ocean at sunset? A kite dancing in a clear blue sky? Perhaps it was a garden you passed on your walk this morning or a beautiful piece of art or music that soothed your soul.

Helen Keller had it right when she said, "The best and most beautiful things in the world cannot be seen or even touched. They must be felt with the heart." Beauty can be found everywhere: in people, food, books, films, music, nature, works of art, etc. Its prolific presence surrounds us, but it often goes unappreciated because we rarely slow down enough to take notice.

In today's culture, the media and so-called internet "influencers" often try to reduce the concept of beauty to a person's physical attributes and style, but beauty runs deeper than our exterior, and it radiates from the inside. You don't need to be wealthy or physically attractive to be beautiful. Beauty shows up through the unique and special qualities that quietly pull others to stand in your light.

Beauty is perceived differently by each of us based on our past experiences, personal preferences, and what we find appealing. What we believe to be beautiful reveals who we are. It can appear when we least expect it: the smell of a family recipe that reminds us of home, a rainbow over a busy skyline that causes us to reset, the innocence of a small child, or an exhibition by our favorite artist.

It's important we nourish our souls by "stopping to smell the roses" rather than rushing by moments of beauty. This week, look around, catch your breath, and simply notice. Here are some suggestions, lest you forget:

1. Pour a bubble bath and think of at least five things that you find beautiful and a time when you experienced each. Remember how you felt each time.

2. Go on an adventure with your partner to look for beauty in the most unlikely places. Share why different things resonate with each of you and what you find beautiful about each.

3. Remind someone about their internal beauty by giving them a card with their name on it and then listing one special quality they have using each letter.

4. Reflect on the adversities you have overcome and the lessons you have learned along the way. Consider how your life has become better and more beautiful because of every experience.

5. Go through your photos and find a handful that you think are beautiful. Print copies and create greeting cards with inspirational notes to uplift friends when they are ill or sad.

6. Step away from the computer, stow the smartphone, and take breaks to notice your surroundings. Each evening, write about beautiful things you saw or heard during your day and why they touched you.

7. Create awareness by spending some time with a child looking through photography and art books. Talk about pictures they think are beautiful and why.

8. Discover beauty by creating beauty. Take a flower arranging

class. Share your newfound knowledge and leave a bouquet of spring flowers on a neighbor's doorstep.

9. Take a moment to listen to the music of nature when you go for a walk. If music stills your heart, make plans to go to a concert and share your "zen" with a friend.

10. Read about the heart and heritage of your favorite dishes and share them with friends at a dinner party or consider writing a family cookbook.

Notes:

Equality

Evening the playing field has been a central theme in my life since I was five. Growing up in Latin America, I witnessed extreme poverty from a very early age, and the image of small children with outstretched hands, or the disabled left to beg on street corners, left an indelible imprint on me that has influenced how I navigate my life.

This theme has remained at the forefront of my thoughts as I was one of only six women in my law school class and, quite frequently, the only woman in senior management roles. Later, as a single mother and entrepreneur, I found a new set of challenges that reminded me that we are not all thought of as equal, particularly when the bias is about the color of our skin, our physical makeup, our marital and economic status, or our age.

With a focus on social rights initiatives in recent years that directly affects recruitment and retention efforts, many companies are hiring professionals to lead diversity, equity, and inclusion programs. Further, laws are being enacted requiring diversity on boards, and there is a continuous flow of human rights movements making the daily news. There is a difference, however, between equality and diversity.

Equality involves ensuring that everyone has equal opportunities and is not treated differently because of certain characteristics, whereas diversity involves considering the differences between people and valuing these differences as a positive.

When was the last time you thought about why every individual should be treated with equal dignity and respect, regardless of their race, gender, religion, sexual orientation, socioeconomic status, or any other defining characteristic? Certainly, the news keeps the topic up front and center, but is the topic of equality relevant to your personal circumstances? Perhaps you feel you don't have either diversity or equality issues, but knowing that others do, does it cause you to feel more empathetic toward them?

For me, the simple answer is that when everyone's voice is heard and their rights are protected, and when each person has access to the same opportunities, resources, and education, then our society will reflect a world that promotes social harmony, dignity, respect, and peace. Community members will feel valued and included by contributing in their own unique ways, judged on their merit and abilities rather than on their backgrounds or circumstances.

Ultimately, equality means that everyone should be able to live the life that makes them happy and fulfilled. We can each contribute to that dream through acceptance, support, and love. Here are some ideas:

1. Take your children or grandchildren to diverse cultural events including movies, concerts, ethnic fairs, food tastings, and different kinds of religious celebrations. Encourage your children to question stereotypes and biases and to think empathetically.

2. Provide resources to those who are at a disadvantage—become a mentor, get involved in local skills training programs, or donate to a scholarship or grant program.

3. If you have a particular calling such as law or accounting, work at pro bono clinics and help those who would not ordinarily be able to afford your services. If you own a hair salon or clothing store, consider a makeover day for those looking for work.

4. Join an organization that supports diversity and inclusion, one that advocates for equal rights and opportunities and shows solidarity with their efforts.

5. Reframe old stories by watching or reading nontraditional fairy tales with your children or grandchildren where the princess doesn't need rescuing, the mother doesn't die and the children outwit the witches and wolves.

6. Educate yourself about something you feel ill-equipped to speak about. Consider food insecurity in your city, microfinance as a poverty alleviation tool, the state of education in your community, the effects of minorities on boards, the unsheltered, etc.

7. Volunteer as a teacher's aide at an elementary school and model inclusivity. Children learn by observing the behavior of those around them, and this is your opportunity to practice and encourage empathy.

8. If you see bias, challenge it! Speak out against discriminatory language or actions by calling out inappropriate behavior and educating yourself and others about different cultures and perspectives.

9. Study and vote for candidates who support equality. Go one step further and get involved with their campaigns.

10. Access to healthcare or the ability to pay for necessary medications is a challenge many of your neighbors face every day. Explore how you can help alleviate this issue.

Notes:

Flexibility

Change can be tough. It can be hard to know where and how to adjust when we are faced with unexpected circumstances. Yet, over the last few years, flexibility has become more important than ever in both our home and business lives. We have been forced to pivot and then pivot again with climate change events, a pandemic, and a struggling marketplace.

We have watched fleet-footed, innovative companies sway like saplings and withstand the winds of change by rethinking supply chains, delivery mechanisms, and product lines. And, sadly, we have said goodbye to others who were resistant to change with little strategic foresight, often unprepared and surprised. The financial penalties for being stuck were steep.

Personally, I've always found that when I hang on perilously to the reeds on the banks while in a boat in fast-flowing water, I end up overboard and drenched, wishing I had just ridden the current to see what was up ahead. Being flexible may require us to have no clear view of the destination, which can be both scary and thrilling.

While we might not be able to control an unexpected turn of events, we can control how we react to it. Mental flexibility sometimes feels like mental gymnastics, but it's an important life skill to master and allows us to calmly evaluate the situation and be open to new ideas. Flexibility is the stepping stone to resilience. It is the *ability* to shift and tack when the winds change. Resilience is a *quality* achieved after navigating through layers and layers of experiences requiring flexibility and the will to survive and thrive.

Fortunately, change gives us the opportunity for "do-overs." I read a quote by John Maxwell: "Change is inevitable. Growth is optional." Do you feel like you have changed and become more adaptable these last few years? Still a ways to go? Here are a few suggestions of ways you can practice and improve flexible thinking and adaptability this week:

1. Learn a new language or teach English in second language classes to increase your mental flexibility as you toggle between languages.

2. Join the Wordle frenzy or pick up a crossword puzzle each morning along with your first cup of coffee to get the gears going. Or try to beat the contestants at Jeopardy or other nightly game shows to shake off the day and test your skills.

3. Change your daily routine. Get up earlier, take a different path on your walk, use a new ingredient, add a new type of exercise, or experiment with a new hobby.

4. Go on a Sunday drive without a planned destination and stop along the way to explore at least two sights that you have never seen before.

5. We all have self-imposed rules—a product of our upbringing. Today, break one of your rules. Widen your boundaries and allow for new experiences! Remember, most of these rules have nothing to do with legal rules; we often create our own enclosures.

6. Survey your friends and co-workers and ask them whether they think you are easy to work or interact with or if they find you rigid. If rigid, think about how that presents itself and how you can modify your behavior.

7. As we age, we can often get stuck in our routines. Does that sound like you or someone you know? Make a list of the

routines you follow each day and ways that you can break the shackles even if it feels uncomfortable.

8. Take an abstract art class with a friend and paint freely without structure.

9. Fear of the unknown and change can be paralyzing. Make a list of irrational fears that you have had in the past that never materialized and what their outcomes were. In the future, can you anticipate the change and begin planning for it in advance so you feel more in control?

10. Join a volunteer or mission trip to a foreign country or with a population that you have very little in common with to broaden your cultural instincts and empathy.

Notes:

Charity

It's easy to question your value when you have been in the job market for a while, have experienced age, gender, or racial discrimination, or have become attached to the idea that your value is represented only by your financial worth. We can become myopic in our quest to increase our bank account and set aside the notion that emotional, social, intellectual, or spiritual values are additional reflections of our worth.

Most people equate volunteer efforts as "feel good" time used to offset the drudgery of paid work. We rarely stop to acknowledge that this contributed time has financial value. (The estimated value of a volunteer's time averages $27 per hour.) When we provide valuable community services, more money is available to be spent on local improvements that we indirectly enjoy. It's a direct contribution to the organization's bottom line and the "universal pot" from which we as active members draw from.

Often, we only make time to volunteer when we have retired or find ourselves in between paid jobs. In moments where our self-esteem is being chipped away, organizations that subsist with volunteer efforts are sincerely happy to have us as part of their team. With very little time contribution, we are gifted a healthy boost to our self-confidence and pride. It's time well spent that allows us to return to our job search and families with a better attitude as we forge ahead. And, we may even learn job skills that will help in our search for financially rewarding work.

For those of us who have retired or who live alone, volunteering can be a boost to our sense of community, allowing us to connect with people and ideas when we aren't quite sure where we fit into the world anymore. We gain new perspectives and, if we are lucky, a new sense of purpose.

This week is a perfect time to give more meaning to your life by adding value to organizations that could really use your help. Consider volunteer efforts as part of your daily routine—not just when your heart needs a lift. Below are some ideas to think about:

1. Donate an old car to the *Disabled Veterans Employment Network* or *Wheels for Wishes*. They will arrange to pick it up, handle the paperwork, and give you a tax receipt to show their appreciation.

2. Go on culinary adventures to restaurants that are social enterprises that offer job training or support causes. Enjoy great food and a unique dining experience.

3. Turn your home into an art gallery for a fun evening. Invite local artists to showcase their art to your family and friends with a percentage of the sales being donated to a local arts education organization.

4. Consider supporting a cause or charity that moves you through crowdfunding sites such as GoFundMe, Fundly, or Chuffed. The choices are many!

5. Become a hospice volunteer and spend time listening to and memorializing the stories of the people who are going through their final days so they know their life's efforts will not be forgotten.

6. Facebook and other social media platforms are great places to redirect unneeded birthday and holiday gifts by asking for charity donations to an organization you want to support.

7. Invite your family and friends to a series of home screenings of documentaries on timely topics and charge an entrance fee that will be donated to a cause you support. Check out The Why

Foundation for ideas.

8. Enjoy the camaraderie of like-minded people doing volunteer work sorting food at a local food bank, constructing a home for a worthy family, or making a wish come true for a child undergoing treatment for a life-threatening illness.

9. Learn to be a pet handler or train your own sweet pet to be a therapy animal with Pet Partners. They bring comfort to people who are facing obstacles.

10. Include a charity contribution in your will as an easy and emotionally fulfilling way to give back but still ensure you have enough money while you are alive.

Notes:

Family

amily means different things to each of us. Some think of family as the relatives that share their home or their lives. Others view their circle of friends or their beloved pets as family. The composition of a family can be vastly different, but happy families all share the same attributes: love and commitment to each other. These are the people who will circle the wagons in stressful times to take care of each other.

Family is essential for providing the love and security that children need to develop into productive, well-balanced adults. It "takes a village" to raise a child, and that includes the many people who teach us the skills we need to face the challenges and adventures ahead. Not having a family because members have died or become estranged can be difficult and isolating for a child. It's the community around them that will influence their success or failure.

Many older people who live alone find themselves in a constant state of fear. They believe they no longer have a safety net in cases of emergency or for financial/emotional support. They lose friends all the time due to illness or relocation to be closer to family, and their sense of isolation and depression is real. It is often exacerbated by social media, where most people only post happy pictures—rarely ones of day-to-day life with all of its challenges or tedium. It can be depressing to watch from afar, and it may even be farther from the truth.

If you have a strong and supportive family, count your blessings. If you don't have a biological family, it's not too late to build a loving and supportive community that will show up as your family of choice. You may find others who are also alone—those who wish for deeper connections. After all, each of us needs a circle of love. Here are a few ideas to help you create a loving support network for yourself or others:

1. Write a letter to a relative that has left a positive impact on you and tell them how much they mean to you and how grateful you are for their presence in your life.

2. Mentor a child at an orphanage or be a Big Brother/Big Sister to an adolescent who may be struggling in a disadvantaged home.

3. Mow the lawn or shovel the driveway for an elderly couple in your neighborhood. Their children may live in another state.

4. Journal about the values and qualities you seek in a chosen family if you do not have one or are estranged from your biological family. Be clear about why each item is important to you.

5. Share your favorite hobby with a nursing home resident who may feel forgotten or whose family is unable to visit with any regularity.

6. Extend your support to a single mother in your neighborhood who is having a hard time navigating parenting alone. Offer to help with meal preparation, tutoring, homework assignments, running errands, or chauffeuring.

7. Do your best to gather the tribe at evening meals. At least once a week, prepare a favorite meal to talk about the best and worst things that happened during the week with each member.

8. Comfort or offer companionship to someone who has suddenly become alone through divorce or the death of a loved one by listening to them and offering a safe place to confide their fears and sadness.

9. Many families and individuals are in a state of flux these days, being forced out of their homes because of wars they had nothing to do with. Most have left their extended families behind. Reach out and show them the meaning of community and what family means to you.

10. If you are feeling isolated and wishing you had a sense of family, start engaging with others through your spiritual community, taking classes to complete a degree you did not finish, or joining meetups or networking associations with people interested in the same things as you. The hardest part is the first step!

Notes:

Health

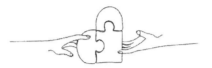

Good health, both physical and emotional, is directly linked to leading a productive life. It is both our greatest gift and asset, as it allows us to do the things that bring us joy, opens the door to more varied opportunities, and ensures our independence for as long as possible.

Optimal health is a key component to handling stress, which is on the rise around the world. The concept of health is not just relegated to physical and mental well-being. People with better financial health often worry less about finances and have additional opportunities to focus on nutrition and regular exercise. Those who enjoy a spiritual commitment may approach life with a sense of calm and purpose that supports their mental health.

Health is a state of complete physical, mental, and social well-being—not merely the absence of disease or infirmity. What is ideal health for you and your loved ones and how can you affect change to ensure your, and their, personal best? As with everything we do, it's important we are balanced in our efforts to stay in good health and not hurting more than helping our bodies and spirits.

Negative effects show up in extreme diets with up and down weight loss, intense sports activities that we have not been conditioned for, or ignoring routine medical exams that monitor our well-being. Sadly, the media and beauty businesses have created an image of what is socially acceptable in terms of appearance to sell more products and services. This has created insecurity among many people who strive to meet those standards—even at the risk of their physical and emotional health.

Living a healthy lifestyle can prevent some chronic diseases and long-term illnesses. Everyone has a unique body with distinctive features, and our needs are all different. Some of us may have issues with weight loss, others with heart health, joint issues, memory loss, or brain health. Our bodies are complex and unique. Peak performance is different for each of us. Below are some ideas to think about as you focus on better health this week.

1. Has it been a while since you had an annual physical? Get a baseline evaluation of your overall health so you can better understand where you might need to focus your attention to be at your best.

2. Speak out against body shaming and bullying in your local schools to prevent school-age kids from having a negative self-image that can last a lifetime. Check in with yourself about negative self-talk.

3. Review what you eat/drink and make the changes required to fuel your body with quality food. Fresh is best, with local fruit and veggies at the top of the list. Consider meeting with a dietician who can create a custom plan for you and your family.

4. Compliment a friend or family member on something not related to their body and ask them what is going on in their life. Keep your focus on the internal qualities that make them unique and special.

5. Track your sleep with a sleep timer on your phone. Most adults need at least seven hours or more of sleep every night to help repair their bodies. Not there? Do some research and learn about ways you can get better rest.

6. Go through your wardrobe and make sure that you have clothes that fit, ones that make you feel like you are at your best. Donate those that don't fit to a friend or organization like *Dress for Success*.

7. Join a food coop at your local farmer's market and share the abundance with an elderly neighbor who may be less mobile. Or, try planting your own garden.

8. Join a Pilates class or a gym with a friend or spouse and include strength training in your weekly exercise routine to keep your bones strong and healthy.

9. Research neighborhoods in "food deserts" and see how you can help. Get involved with community and school gardens that both teach food health and provide nutritious vegetables to students.

10. Take a walk each morning with friends and make it a daily wellness event. The first step you take each day can be the beginning of a brand-new you!

Notes:

Entrepreneurism

I love the entrepreneurial spirit—the can-do spirit of dreamers! They thrive on curiosity and the desire to make things better. They offer answers that are new and different and are "Solutionaries." They take risks to follow their passion, optimistic about their future and their impact. They hope to move the needle.

Although many people only dream of having their own business, others may be forced into action to make it a reality because of personal challenges that move the timeline up. Sudden change can be scary, but history shows that innovation always peaks when people are forced to pivot and think of resolutions to problems they did not see coming. During those times, we have made some of the biggest social advances for humanity.

Post-pandemic, many of those leaving W-2 jobs have decided they need to make it on their own rather than rely on someone else. With a heightened sense of urgency because of extreme weather events, the rise of social issues such as homelessness and food insecurity, and a need for rapid and innovative solutions, they are leading the charge to create products and services that will serve the world well. These are all hallmarks of social entrepreneurs and a rise in ethical consumerism.

I often say that I would be a rich woman if I could sell each of my ideas for a nickel. But, it's the execution that counts, not just the ideas, and it's our entrepreneurs who take a great idea and make it happen by implementing it. It takes guts to put yourself out there.

We could all use cheerleaders. Below are some ideas to lend the entrepreneurs a hand:

1. Support a local business by purchasing their products/services, giving referrals, helping them make a sale, or giving them a shout-out on social media outlets such as Yelp, Facebook, or LinkedIn.

2. Small businesses often rely on family and friends for seed capital. Consider becoming an angel investor, donating to help them launch their dream, or introducing them to funding sources.

3. Help a farmer by shopping at the farmers market and preparing meals with organic foods. Consider buying a membership to a farmers' cooperative and have produce or meat regularly delivered directly to your home.

4. Social enterprises are businesses created to offer social benefits in addition to making a profit. If you are interested in helping a business whose mission is to make our world a better place to live in, your skills, talents, and enthusiasm will be appreciated!

5. Offer minority-owned businesses discounts or other opportunities to encourage their success. Consider hiring them as your vendors for SEO/web, legal, accounting, cleaning, hair, dental, and other personal services.

6. Become a Junior Achievement volunteer. You might enjoy educating students from elementary school through high school about life skills, personal finances, budgeting, available careers, or starting and running a business.

7. Invite entrepreneurs to local meetups, business networking events, seminars, conferences, and webinars—any place that will showcase their product/service and expand their circle of influence. Introduce them to possible alliance partners and potential advisory board members to help contribute to their success.

8. If you are a retired executive, join SCORE, a small business mentoring organization with almost 400 chapters. Offer your services to startups looking for a mentor and guide as they launch their passion. Or consider sharing your wisdom at a small business incubator, which is always looking for talent like yours.

9. Entrepreneurship can be lonely. Consider joining a co-working space with other entrepreneurs for companionship and general support. Spaces are geared to a variety of industries and even to different genders—if, for instance, you are more comfortable in a woman-owned business setting.

10. Don't forget our youth entrepreneurs. They are our future! Get involved with Lemonade Day a fun, experiential program that teaches youth how to start, own, and operate their very own business—a lemonade stand. Or check out Build, which teaches underserved high school students how to start their own businesses. The options are endless!

Notes:

Communication

Though some of us are born with "the gift of gab," it takes most of us years to learn how to better our abilities to both share and receive information from others. We start as toddlers mimicking words that our parents read to us from picture books and continue the journey in elementary school by practicing our reading and writing skills. Throughout high school, we research and write papers for grades, participate in speech and debate contests, and run for student government.

We learn that being able to state our position and articulate its importance in a way that others will hear and understand is a valuable skill set. It's a path to getting what we want. For this exchange of information to be rewarding to both parties, we must be as committed to listening as we are to speaking. After all, communication runs both ways. Words only matter if there is someone to hear them—a person invested in listening to the point we are trying to make.

There is an art to effective communication. We can't truly connect with another person if we are multitasking or on our phones, busy reacting to incessant sound notifications. And, we aren't giving others our full attention if we are "stepping on" their words to hear our own voices or are busy thinking about the next thing we will say before the other person finishes. A good communicator is focused and respectful.

I have found that nonverbal communication is just as informative as the use of words. The way we move and carry ourselves communicates a wealth of information to the world. Our level of confidence is conveyed by our posture, stance, and gait just as our handshakes project weakness or control. If we infringe on people's personal space, it can be perceived as a reflection of aggression or dominance. Are their arms crossed, are they tapping their feet or avoiding eye contact? Are they backing away from you if you move closer in your enthusiasm or stepping toward you to share more intimacy?

Paying attention to these aspects of our lives yields valuable information that can make our relationships more rewarding. Here are some suggestions to think about this week:

1. Practice your listening skills by showing interest and asking questions of others. Paraphrase what you have heard and ask for clarification or more information.

2. Join a Toastmasters club to become a better and more confident speaker. There are almost 15,000 clubs in 145 countries to choose from.

3. Tone is an important part of successful communication. Be aware of your tone, particularly if you are annoyed with someone. Is it in your best interest to sound patronizing or short? Will your point go unheard?

4. Write a paragraph about your personal brand—what people say about you when you leave the room. Are your actions consistent with your words?

5. Many relationships have suffered due to texts. Think about the times you have had an issue because of texting and why. Would you do anything different?

6. Invite friends over for your own TED Talk party and watch great speakers share their ideas. Then discuss what you learned and how you feel about the topic. Or attend a TED conference and consider applying to give a speech of your own!

7. Check your email messages before you hit send. Are they brief

and specific with accurate grammar and spelling? Pause when you are angry or emotional and hold off sending the message until the following day.

8. Volunteer to be a judge at a speech contest or attend a pitch for business funding. Knowing what to look for will help your own presentations be more effective.

9. Help a teen create a storybook of some of the most fun or interesting things that have happened in their life. These examples will help them break the ice when they are meeting new people or joining clubs and organizations.

10. Create a list of 10 ways that you can turn small talk into a real conversation. Make sure that the weather is not one of those topics!

Notes:

Tolerance

I often wonder what the world would be like if we were more tolerant of each other's beliefs and less judgmental. What if we remained in our lane or widened it for others we might not "get" but who seek a path forward to happiness and peace like most of humanity?

We are often asked and expected to accept and embrace that which we don't understand. Someone else's social conditioning may contradict ours, and they may be raised in different communities with different religions and political standards. Every family has their own culture and traditions, and acceptance may be out of their social confines or comfort zone. Often, this is revealed through the lack of education and empathy.

The ability to "be" with others despite our differences or emotions reflects our tolerance quotient and our courage. It's not about abandoning our own beliefs or convictions; it's about holding space for others to have theirs. It isn't always easy, and it requires respect, empathy, and approaching every interaction with an open mind and willing heart.

Do you foster unguarded communication and discussion with others by educating yourself on different viewpoints? Do you grow and express tolerance in positive ways? Acknowledging the viewpoints of others is an essential skill in the workplace, the classroom, at home, and in public spaces. Ultimately, tolerance is about accepting people who have different abilities, interests, and styles without judgment—but that does not mean that you must accept bad behavior beyond what is socially acceptable.

We are given many opportunities each day for self-reflection about our limitations and the labels we place on people or issues. Judgment, after all, serves no purpose even though it can be challenging with so many different cultures, backgrounds, and, frankly, annoying people around us! Life is interesting and diverse. Below are a handful of ideas and ways that you can practice tolerance this week:

1. Improve self-awareness by understanding your values. They impact how you filter and process information about people and circumstances. Can you think of ways that your life experiences regarding race, gender, or religion have defined how you view and react to others? Reflection is a bridge to a broader perspective.

2. Cultivate the spiritual practice of meditation and start with 5-10 minutes each day. Need a little help to get going? Check out Mindful.org or Deepak Chopra's guided meditations.

3. Support a cause, movement, or organization aimed at leveling the playing field for all. Historical ones include the NAACP and ACLU, and there are many new ones including Race Forward, The Transgender Law Center, and Fair Fight. Many corporations have minority initiatives, as do committees at service organizations.

4. At least once weekly, experience other people's traditions and religions. From trying a new ethnic recipe to attending a religious service different than your own, take the time to learn.

5. Have political discussions not to take a stance or convince others of your ways but to learn why people have their own beliefs. By doing this, you can find ways to meet in the middle when you are diametrically opposed.

6. If you feel yourself judging a situation or a person today, suspend judgment, check your ego, pause, and actively listen to their position. You don't know what they are facing or what is going on behind the scenes.

7. Talk to women about dress codes in their country (90 percent of clothing bans are associated with women) and how they feel about them without expressing an opinion.

8. Develop curiosity and travel to places new and different. They may seem exotic to you, but they are home to someone. Embracing another culture and lifestyle creates empathy and tolerance.

9. Are you a NIMBY (an upper-middle-class person who opposes affordable housing or racial diversity in their neighborhood) or a YIMBY (people who say they want a more diverse neighborhood in terms of both class and race and who support affordable housing initiatives in their neighborhoods)?

10. Own your feelings and recognize that no one can make you feel a certain way without your permission.

Notes:

Touch

Human attention and touch, it turns out, is essential for maintaining our mental and physical health. This was especially apparent during the COVID-19 pandemic when human touch was discouraged. Many of us suffered trauma and "skin hunger" from a lack of contact with other humans, effects that are still being felt today, long after isolation has ended.

The moment a baby is born, it is embraced and held close—the beginning of a life filled with biological stimulation that plays an essential role in a child's development. A pat on the back and rocking can soothe and lower stress in babies, and, as they get older, a reassuring hug or an outstretched hand can contribute to a sense of security and calm.

Premature babies, housed in the NICU of hospital nurseries, may associate their feedings with tubes and wires, so being held is vitally important for them to build a positive association with eating. We know that low birth-weight infants gain weight faster when they receive skin-to-skin contact from their parents, and volunteer baby cuddlers are welcomed by overworked nurses.

At the other end of life's journey, studies have shown that the elderly receive the least amount of touching of any age group due to social isolation. Yet, it is vitally important for these older adults who may be suffering from depression and chronic illness. A simple hug or pat on the hand can help alleviate their feelings of fear and loneliness and show them that someone cares, which increases alertness, memory, and cognitive functions. It also lowers blood pressure and reduces anxiety and stress—all leading to a healthier and longer life.

Physical touch is the most direct and intimate way to connect with others, which is why our first inclination at hearing that someone is troubled is to give them a hug. It comes naturally to us. We want them to feel better. Take time this week to reach out and experience the gift of touch, something we no longer take for granted. Here are a few ideas to get you started:

1. Do a volunteer project at your local humane society and enjoy the company of lonely pets that would welcome some attention and cuddling from you. Consider adding one to the family!

2. Take an essential oil class and learn about the different benefits of each fragrance. Then create your own custom bath spray and enjoy how it feels as you massage it into your skin.

3. While you sit at your desk or watch TV, gently but firmly roll your feet across a tennis ball, massage ball, or foam roller to release tension.

4. Teach a young person how to correctly shake hands with sustained eye contact to show confidence and warmth.

5. Redo your bedding with the most luxurious sheets you can afford. Consider a weighted blanket for a dreamy embrace and a solid night's sleep.

6. Play catch, tickle, or wrestle with your child or grandchild and enjoy their laughter and sweet innocence.

7. Time for a new hairstyle? There is nothing better than having a scalp massage and having someone brush your hair. Not only does it feel great, but it also brings blood to your scalp and promotes hair growth and fullness.

8. Host a tranquil at-home spa day for your friends. Start with an oil diffuser, scented candles, a calming playlist, and healthy snacks. Tell everyone to wear comfy clothes, bring their furry slippers, and leave their cell phones in the car. Consider hiring a massage therapist to come in for the afternoon as a special treat.

9. Realize that if you are reading this, you survived a global pandemic and could probably use a good hug from someone who could also use the comfort of one. Be generous with your hugs, and be thankful that they are free and precious!

10. From the beginning to the end, we all need to be touched. Volunteer to comfort babies in the NICU of your local hospital as a baby cuddler or spend time holding the hand of an elderly person at a senior center who could use a friend.

Notes:

Friendship

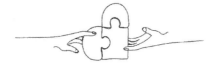

Humans are social beings. We all crave friendship. But, making enduring friendships as we get older isn't as easy as when we were children. A May 2021 American Perspectives survey found that many Americans have very few close friends. Instead, they have situational friendships—temporary friendships made at work, in a class, or in some other shared community. So, why are adult friendships so difficult to establish?

Our childhood friendships revolved around fun and adventure! We went to the same school, played team sports, and listened to trendy music. We did almost everything together as we discovered the world around us. That same type of bond was equally strong with our roommates from college or our first apartment as we moved into adulthood together.

Life in today's world is hectic, and available time is a big factor. Many of us now work longer hours, travel greater distances to work, and have children later in life with added family responsibilities. Add in a global pandemic that threw us all into social isolation for a few years, and we have a recipe for unwelcome solitude.

As the years go by, close friendships often get tested or fade away. We may try to stay in touch, but distance and the lack of social interaction make it difficult to hold on to the closeness we once had. And, as we age with a lifetime of experiences, we may find it harder to put our trust in someone new and fully invest in them as a friend the way we did as a child. Fear of being disappointed or hurt by friends can easily stop you from getting close.

It's important to remember that the new friend of today may one day be the old friend that we have shared our joys and sorrows with if we only give the friendship a chance. This week, discover how you can meet and make new friends and maintain strong, mutually supportive relationships—with a little tending. Here are some ideas:

1. Join a civic-minded organization like Rotary or Lions Club, where you can make new friends while you make a positive impact on others.

2. Lost touch with an old friend? Do a little research and try reconnecting through a social media site. Life gets in the way, but old friends enjoy reminiscing about "the good ol' days!"

3. Get to know your neighbors better with a backyard cookout or a potluck dinner. This is a great way for both young and old to connect.

4. There are many hallmarks to being a great friend. Call someone and tell them you're thinking of them or send them a card to brighten their day and make them feel special.

5. It can be tough to travel if you are single and prone to loneliness. Research and sign up for a group trip with other singles to a place you've never been before. Some of the best friends are made on adventures!

6. Create new friendships by expanding your circle with friends of friends. It can be convenient and safe because they often share many of the same interests and characteristics as your mutual friend.

7. Love to read? Join one or more local book clubs and choose interesting reading materials with kindred spirits who have the same passion. Enjoy discussing the things you loved and hated about each book and find commonalities.

8. Athletic or trying to stay in shape? Join a hiking club, invite a friend to a yoga class, or explore the latest Pickleball fad with other fans.

9. Join a Meetup group exploring almost any topic you can think of. Just type in your favorite hobby in a search engine and a list of groups in your area will pop up with a variety of events they are participating in or creating. Or start your own group and be surprised by the interest!

10. Invite acquaintances or new friends to your home for a home-cooked meal. It can be fun to have a theme such as a Galentine's Day brunch or a Kentucky Derby afternoon mixer to create a festive air. Or, lead a cooking class by trying new recipes or unusual ingredients that you might not normally cook at home.

Notes:

Ageism

The graying of the world's population is no longer a futuristic prediction: The Beatles launched their trip to fame on *The Ed Sullivan Show* over 50 years ago, and their groupies, the Baby Boomers, are moving into their 70s. The longest-living generation in history, this group of people is known for their strong work ethic, resourcefulness, competitiveness, and discipline. They have created lasting business relationships for decades and amassed a high net worth.

So, imagine their rude awakening to discover that the media and society, in general, continue to uphold the myth that anyone over the age of 60 is frail, feeble, losing their mental acuities, and financially distressed—basically a burden to society. But…that's just not the case in most instances. Many are just starting their "third trimester" and look forward to new businesses, new marriages, travel to exotic locations, and retooling with classes and education. They lead rich and fulfilled lives.

The one thing that does ring true for this population, and many of the other generations post-pandemic, is that loneliness and a sense of isolation have become prevalent. Faced with workforce discrimination, partners passing away, children moving to other geographic locations as they follow their own dreams and desires, health issues, and an overwhelming sense that they no longer add value is causing mental health challenges and suicide rates to increase. Men aged 85 and older have the highest rate of suicide of any group in the country.

So, what's the answer? After all, they are still contributing through their consumer spending, generous charitable donations, and corporate investments. Many have picked up family obligations, raising grandchildren when they thought they would be traveling the world and enjoying the fruits of their labor. With life expectancy increasing, they need and want to be able to contribute in meaningful ways.

Let's start with the idea that "old age" is a social concept rather than a true biological one—that there is no clearly defined and universally valid threshold that marks old age. Can we strip away the label and see each person for the unique gifts and talents they offer? Below are some ways that you help with this socially pressing issue.

1. Host a viewing party for the documentary *Lives Well Lived*. It's a reminder that age is just a number!

2. Participate in advocacy work to ensure your rights are protected in the workforce or that you aren't lost in the healthcare system. Check out the advocacy programs at AARP, The National Council on Aging, and Generations United.

3. Many museums offer day trips to visit sister museums in neighboring cities. Join a group of seniors and other individuals interested in learning more about the arts.

4. Create a plan to help your elderly family members *age in place*. The NIH (National Institute on Health) offers many resources to help each of us stay in our homes for as long as possible.

5. Many Boomers are actively looking for work and facing discrimination with software filters that cull them based on age. Provide a referral or offer to help them update their social media profiles to help them overcome these obstacles.

6. Pet sit for a senior who may have the opportunity to go visit family or friends or who find themselves staying overnight at a hospital. Their pet may be their closest companion. Let them know they are being well taken care of and loved.

7. Interested in a new business that will leave a lasting impact? Many Boomers are creating legacy businesses to help solve issues facing our world. Consider using your network and funds to create a social enterprise that will fill your heart account as full as your bank account.

8. Share your wisdom with seniors at a retirement community. Teach an individual or seniors' group computer, internet, and social media skills—or something fun like art history, cooking, or a workshop about publishing a book.

9. Consider creating a shared site that brings children and seniors together for human contact and positive role models. Check out Sharing Our Space.

10. Become a certified senior manager or geriatric care manager. These professionals are especially helpful when family members live far apart and their loved one needs assistance.

Notes:

Honesty

In a world filled with media untruths and stories slanted toward high drama, it can be hard to discern what is truthful and what is not. It's discouraging because we all want transparent relationships, personal or otherwise. So, how can we find and build trust with others—growing relationships that are based on openness and mutual respect?

Expressing ourselves authentically and freely and listening to others without judgment or bias are the cornerstones of trust. We find out quickly where we stand by their reaction to our words and actions—whether they trust and rely upon us or they believe we have misled them or been untruthful. Sadly, once we have broken their trust and the seed of doubt has been planted, it's very difficult to regain confidence.

Where does the line begin and end between "I'm sorry, I have other plans" when you don't and habitual deception? Ask yourself if the other person would have felt deceived if they knew. Probably. It's a risk sometimes to tell others how we really feel, and it can be scary, but the alternative is not being true to ourselves or them. It's the small skewing of the truth that colors our ability to live a fully authentic life.

Most of us want to believe that we are honest, truthful, transparent, and straightforward in our actions and words. As parents, it's one of the first lessons we teach our children. It is a foundational pillar of our wedding vows, and the underpinnings of many marriages have been broken once a lie has been revealed. And, if we are not true to our word in our career, we are immediately labeled as an employee or businessperson with a lack of integrity.

Honesty is one of the building blocks of trust and respect and a hallmark of integrity. Our personal growth is dependent on self-respect. Do we like the person we see in the mirror? Are we living a life that we are proud of, one that brings us joy, or deluding ourselves just to please others? Are we staying in a relationship full of deceit because we are afraid to leave? Honesty is not just about the stories we tell others; it's also about the stories we tell ourselves.

This week, take some time to peel the onion back on your relationship with yourself and others. Here are some thoughts.

1. Take inventory of the promises, or offers, you've made to others. Are there a few you have not kept? Identify those instances and work on fulfilling those promises.

2. Journal about "your story," the one you tell others and yourself. Are you being 100 percent honest or is it skewed to make yourself feel better?

3. Practice providing colleagues or friends with honest constructive feedback in a way they can hear without feeling hurt to improve their situation.

4. Everyone makes mistakes. Be honest about the ones you make and quickly make amends where necessary. Are you open to forgiving others for theirs?

5. Have a conversation with someone who has lied to you and try to gain clarity about why they felt compelled to lie for both your and their personal growth.

6. Take some time to reflect on your limitations and be honest with yourself about what you can and cannot do. Try saying "No" with straightforward reasons this week.

7. Ask someone you trust for their honest feedback on your work performance and accept their suggestions as constructive with grace and dignity.

8. Have an open and honest conversation with someone who has disappointed you, telling them why without attacking them, understanding your role and theirs.

9. Return anything that belongs to another or repay a loan even if it has been forgotten to breed a sense of integrity and respect.

10. Write down a list of your core values and post it next to your computer. Read over it daily and make sure your daily decisions align with them.

Notes:

Hope

Every day we face choices from challenges that may appear insurmountable. Our destination is often based on our outlook. One path keeps us moving forward and believing that tomorrow will be a better day, whereas the other road inevitably leads to paralysis, fear, or despair. Ultimately, the path we choose affects every aspect of our lives—our relationships, our emotional health, and, quite possibly, our physical health.

Sometimes, despite our best efforts, we find ourselves losing hope—that feeling that ignites our imagination, allowing us to see better days ahead. It's not always easy to dig deep when you have been knocked down a few times or there is no answer in sight. I find that stepping away from the issue is often a solution for me. Perspective is the great equalizer and a wonderful path back to a state of hopefulness. Something as simple as a walk, cleaning out a closet, listening to upbeat music, or having coffee with a friend helps me reset my emotions and gain a new frame of reference.

We know that a hopeful approach to living helps us manage stress and apprehension. It's been shown that belief and expectation, the key elements of hope, can impact our nervous system, which then sets off a chain reaction that can make improvement and recovery more likely. In addition to lowering the risk of developing cardiovascular disease and other chronic conditions, hope has even influenced fundamental physiological processes like respiration, circulation, and motor function.

Hope encourages and inspires us to move forward and act despite the obstacles that lie ahead. Are you a pessimist or an optimist? If you lean toward negativity, does it serve you? Hopeful people believe they can make a positive difference, and it is this belief that can, and very often does, help to make the world a much better place. When we have hope and a clear belief in what's possible, we are more likely to achieve our goals and make our dreams, and those of others, a reality.

Need a little help in seeing the bright side of things or know someone who does? Below are a few suggestions to help you get started:

1. Talk to someone about their dreams and aspirations and share what you learned on your journey. It may help them move forward with greater confidence.

2. Remind someone of their accomplishments if they are feeling defeated and help them create a detailed plan to get unstuck. Check in with them often to gauge their progress and provide positive reinforcement.

3. Take a moment to reflect on where you are and where you want to be in the future. Create a vision board with images to help you get there and place it in a prominent place you can view each day.

4. Establish a nurturing self-care routine that makes you happy. You might go to the gym, take a yoga class, walk on the beach, listen to great music, or get a manicure. Build hope and resilience by stepping out of the hustle and bustle of daily life to take care of yourself.

5. Homelessness breeds hopelessness. Volunteer with an organization that helps the homeless regain their sense of pride so they can find jobs and housing.

6. Limit your bad news intake by taking a break from social media and the daily newscast. Instead, read and share inspiring books or movies to lift everyone up.

7. Lead a journalism workshop for students to create a good news newsletter with articles about amazing founders of innovative companies searching for solutions to some of our world's most pressing issues.

8. To increase your hope for the future, write about something you wished for that was eventually realized and how you felt when it happened.

9. Visit a children's hospital and read stories to the patients. When we give hope to others, we feel better, too. The most sustainable hope is the kind you give away.

10. Hope is a long-term decision that opens the door for good coming into our lives even as we navigate dark days or hard times. Look for it in places you have not thought about before and journal about this search.

Notes:

Imagination

The world of reality has its limits, but the world of imagination has no boundaries! Albert Einstein is remembered as saying, "Imagination is more important than knowledge. For knowledge is limited, whereas imagination embraces the entire world, stimulating progress, giving birth to evolution."

Imagination has been the catalyst for every technological innovation, architectural monument, scientific discovery, movie, book, or poem. It has the extraordinary capacity to shape reality because it permits us to close the door to the outside world and its cacophony and dream about a place where we can leave our imprint. It acts as a motivator, boosting our creativity and enthusiasm to achieve.

Unfortunately, we often lose our childlike imagination as we begin to understand how the world works. We are taught to be practical, focusing on the more serious things in life. We find ourselves lost in the drudgery of household tasks and meeting work obligations, or falling prey to social media and the heaviness of global politics. We may even find AI to be our new source of ideas.

Sadly, there is truth to the warning "use it or lose it." The pump must be primed daily. Even if you believe you can't prove, create, or implement your ideas because others would dismiss them as crazy or impossible, you must imagine what it would be like if you could remain curious, open-minded, and independent.

There is no limit to the human imagination. We have been witness to many people who have believed fiercely in their dreams, refusing to listen to the naysayers. Ultimately, they achieved them, exhausted but fulfilled. This ability of our mind to be creative and resourceful is an amazing life skill that is activated every time we read a book, go down a rabbit trail on the internet, inquire about another person's life, or experiment in the kitchen.

This week, make a conscious effort to spend some time imagining how your world could be different and better. And then, believing it, take a step forward to make some of those dreams come true. More often than not, your thoughts become your reality and a self-proving prophecy, so tweak them if you need to. Here are some ideas:

1. Take a friend to a comedy improv show and consider signing up for a class. Practice thinking on your feet and voicing your ideas, no matter how crazy they may seem.

2. Make up a short story for a child that will inspire him, then share it and have him rewrite the ending.

3. Ask your partner to go with you to a free-style dance class and practice choreographing new moves together.

4. Experiment with creating a new dish without using a recipe. See which ingredients work together for your palate and which don't.

5. Be empathetic to another person's situation today. Imagine what it must be like to be in their shoes, dealing with the challenges they are facing.

6. Read about manifestation or watch *The Secret* if you are interested in quantum physics.

7. Start a Friday night culture club with friends and enjoy theater, movies, art exhibits, and museum field trips. Be inspired by the imagination of others.

8. Plan a trip to somewhere you have never been. Planning is half the fun, so spare no effort in making it an experience to remember.

9. Keep a dream journal if you are an active dreamer and study what your subconscious is telling you while you are asleep. It may not be what you think!

10. Brainstorm with a friend who is interested in starting a new business about the ins and outs of getting it up and running. What is the vision of the founder, their hopes and dreams?

Notes:

Respect

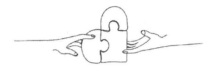

I would be very surprised if you haven't heard and danced to the Aretha Franklin song "Respect." The song became a running anthem for the feminist and civil rights movements throughout the 1970s. The concept of, and the need for, respect, however, endures.

Each of us wants to be accepted for who we are. Though we are uniquely different from others, with varied opinions about those differences, we hope that our views will be valued and given equal consideration. Additionally, we hope to be heard and included in kind with courteous exchanges.

It starts with us. When we are aware of how our language and tone affect others, it shows that we are conscious of and care about our impact. Exhibiting humility and sensitivity, empathizing with different perspectives, following up on our commitments in a timely manner, or sincerely apologizing when we are wrong are all signs of respect.

Unfortunately, an important component of respect that we often forget is self-respect. This means being good to ourselves and taking care of our needs, both physical and emotional. And, being patient—stopping all self-criticism before it turns into a bad habit. Look in the mirror, smile, and pat yourself on the back, acknowledging all your efforts. It will do wonders to break a pattern of behavior that serves no one.

Ultimately, being able to forgive someone who has fallen from grace in our eyes is the truest form of regard for another person's humanity. When we are willing to suspend all judgment and give people the benefit of the doubt, with the belief that most people have good intentions but are human and often fail, we have offered them the opportunity to rise to their best and most respectful selves.

This week, make note of the times you could have been more respectful and the times that you reflected the characteristics of a respectful person. Remember the adage that most people may not remember your words, but they do remember how you made them feel. Below are some ideas:

1. Show hospitality workers that you value their worth and abilities by praising their efforts, tipping generously, and calling them by their names.

2. Be punctual. If you say you're going to be somewhere at 2:00, be there at 2:00, not 2:05. Another person's time is as valuable to them as yours is to you.

3. Sarcasm, group gossip, or teasing has little place in a respectful environment. Pay attention to who is participating. It's generally at the expense of others.

4. Join and get involved with an organization promoting respect such as United for Respect or RespectAbility and show by "walking the walk and talking the talk."

5. Treat yourself in a way that you would want others to treat you, and be conscious of negative self-talk or actions. Each evening before you turn out the lights, write down one thing that you respect about yourself in a bedside journal.

6. Good manners and etiquette are marks of respect. Can you think of ways that you have slacked off and can improve yours?

7. Include others who may be more introverted in a group conversation so they know their thoughts and opinions are equally important. Ask directly for their input and give them time to respond.

8. Be mindful. Hold the door open or give up your seat on the bus to someone who could use this small courtesy.

9. Shine the light on the abilities of a person who is considered disabled. Change the narrative. Be inclusive and encourage their interactions with others.

10. Call out disrespectful behavior when you see it, understanding that, possibly, the person doesn't realize the impact of their behavior. Give them a chance to apologize and be more polite.

Notes:

Compassion

There is a lot of talk about *empathy* these days with a more narrowed focus on diversity and equity. Empathy refers to the general ability to take another person's perspective and feel their emotions. This concept reflects one's ability to "cross the bridge" to understanding and appreciating our differences.

Compassion, on the other hand, is what happens when those feelings of empathy are accompanied by the desire to help if needed and to find a way to change the situation and ease the other person's pain.

The ability to be compassionate can be learned and honed. It isn't a "you have it or you don't" proposition. Learning this ability may take some time and practice, but it's worth it to keep flexing our compassion skills by actively participating—not just momentarily feeling another person's pain and then moving on.

Unfortunately, it's not always so easy to feel the same compassion for ourselves as we do for others. We are told not to be selfish from the time we are small children and to put other's needs first and often, we do so at our own expense. Though we have all heard the admonition from flight attendants to "Put your mask on first before you put one on your child," our natural inclination is to take care of our child's needs before our own.

Still, we are no good to others if we are exhausted and at the end of our rope. Self-care plays an important part in our health and well-being. It allows us to recharge and be in service to others, as well as meet our own needs. And, when we feel good about our actions, we have a renewed sense of purpose and improved relationships. Science even says we live longer! One of the most important things we can do for ourselves is to direct a little of our compassion our own way.

Here are some ways to shine the light on compassion this week:

1. Make a family Kindness Jar and drop a note in with each act of kindness practiced throughout the week. Read the notes at the end of the week over dinner and celebrate each other's good works.

2. Work as a patient advocate at your local hospital. It can be hard to think clearly when ill. We often miss a lot of the information given to us or don't ask the questions we later wish we had. You can be the eyes and ears of another during this time.

3. Before bed, think about the times you judged or criticized another, even mentally, throughout the day. Then ask yourself why and on what basis. Remind yourself that the following day you get a "do-over."

4. Our words hold massive power that impacts recipients in either a positive or negative manner. They can build someone up or tear them down, motivate or discourage them, and make or break someone's day. Have you experienced both? Jot down a few examples.

5. Show acceptance of another by validating their feelings whether you agree or not. Show that you care enough to listen to their story about a situation or person.

6. Be compassionate with yourself by letting go of things and people that don't serve you or add richness to your life. Try not to beat yourself up over your perceived imperfections and give yourself some grace.

7. Do a self-check to see if you are respecting the personal boundaries of family and friends without intrusion, resentment, or feeling rejected. Ask questions to understand what their limits are and watch for non-verbal cues.

8. Lend a helping hand by helping someone pick up their groceries if a bag breaks, aiding an elderly person across the street, assisting a friend when they move, or giving directions to a newcomer to the area.

9. Teach your teens to be happy for someone else's success even if it feels like they lost out. Then, revisit this concept of good sportsmanship yourself. Could there have been instances this week at work where you could have done better at celebrating a co-worker's win?

10. Finally, when other people express compassion for your own hardships, be grateful and say thank you for their love and concern.

Notes:

Grace

Many of us enjoy the ballet. Dancers glide gracefully across the stage with simple elegance and refined movement. Their steps appear effortless as they move fluidly with the music. They are valued partners with the orchestra whose individual instruments have a respected and integral role in the outcome and success of the production. They have each worked hard to work in sync with the others and achieve this harmony.

Life can feel disjointed, full of starts and stops, and we may find ourselves yearning for that type of congruity. So, where and how does the concept of grace fit into our daily lives? Like the dancers, the less attention we pay to the disturbing cacophony of unwelcome chatter to either side of us and the more we focus instead on where our gifts and talents add value and a sense of peace to the world around us, the better chance we have of living in harmony.

Although some might confine the concept of grace to a theological notion narrowed down to Divine Grace and unmerited favors, I would like to think that there is more spaciousness around the word that includes both receiving it from and giving it to others. Grace quiets us and gives us a sense of well-being. It often shows up as second chances, honor, beauty, civility, and decency, and it is a quick way to discard judgment and self-righteousness.

Grace isn't just extended to others but is at its best when we offer it to ourselves because that's when it can be the hardest. When I walk in grace, I try to be kind to myself just as I would be to another who might be struggling. It is best to breathe deeply and accept that life just gets in the way when we least expect it. I try not to sweat the small stuff and know that I'm doing my very best. I've learned that layering on additional pressure and angst serves no purpose.

Have you heard of the South African term *ubuntu,* which means "I am because you are?" It's a reflection of our interdependence as humans and our responsibility to our planet and those who live on it. It reminds us that life is a brightly woven tapestry most beautiful when completed, every thread an integral part. Harmony and grace coexist when we are tuned in to the world, unified though separate. Below are some things to think about this week:

1. Cut at least one person who irritates you or who was rude to you today some slack. You don't know their personal struggles.

2. Pick up the well-known book *The Power of Now* and practice living in the moment rather than worrying about the future or feeling bad about the past.

3. If someone asks for forgiveness, can you accept it graciously, without correction, modification, or embellishment, which qualifies their apology and makes your acceptance of it conditional?

4. Practice self-compassion and give yourself a "Get out of Jail" card today if things don't come together as you had hoped they would.

5. Listen to your teen's explanation of an action gone wrong and show grace and respect by quietly paying attention and asking them what they would have done differently.

6. Practice saying, "Thank you" and showing your appreciation frequently during the day to co-workers, friends, family, and strangers.

7. Ask yourself if you are lifting people up when you offer sage advice or just trying to change or mold them to your perception of a better version.

8. Write down a handful of ways that you see and feel beauty and grace and commit to spending more time seeking them out.

9. Start with kindness. Today, think about your tone and the words you use. Are they collaborative, unifying, and inviting to others to share?

10. Let it go. Are you holding onto grudges whether you are aware of them or not? Bless the person you are upset with and shed this energy-draining burden.

Notes:

Mentoring

We have all been mentored at one time or another, and I bet most of us have acted as a mentor to someone else. These are the people in our lives who have helped us grow and develop—the ones who have experience and provide us with practical knowledge and advice. These connections influence our lives at home, at work, and in our communities.

A mentor can take on many roles: teacher, sponsor, advisor, agent, role model, coach, and confidante. They show up at different times in our lives depending on our needs, age, occupation, or personal quest. For a young person, having a mentor may be life-changing, as their mentor might be the only person in their life they feel they can trust as they navigate the challenges of youth. For someone amid changing careers, navigating the corporate path, or starting a new business, a mentor can shave much-needed time off the learning curve.

There is a yin and a yang to these relationships. If we are the mentors, then these interactions can help us build leadership and management skills, expand our professional network, and provide us with a meaningful way to give back to our communities. If we are the ones being mentored, we may see improvement academically, socially, financially, and in terms of personal fulfillment.

Consider establishing a personal board of mentors, your "kitchen cabinet," each with a particular skill and mindset that will guide you and cheer you on as you navigate the road ahead of you. The success of my own relationships with my mentors has always been based on trust, vulnerability, respect, expectation, and communication. This tapestry of wisdom has enriched my life in ways I never could have foreseen.

The opportunities are wide open for you to get involved in both sharing and learning opportunities. Below are some ways to participate in this give–and–take relationship. Others need your wisdom as much as you need theirs:

1. Check out your local city workforce partnerships. Many have programs that help job seekers find fulfilling work, and they could use your help preparing candidates for interviews, creating better social media profiles, or drafting bios and resumes.

2. Join professional networking organizations and meet a community that you can both share your wisdom with and learn from as you grow your network. Depending on your interests, search for service, industry organizations, or those cause-oriented.

3. If you are looking for a mentor, reach out to your community, either personally or through social media, and tell them about your needs. Be specific.

4. CEOs need mentoring too. Explore Vistage, a CEO peer group tailored to your industry with other experienced CEOS willing to share their expertise, challenges, and solutions.

5. If you have ever been faced with a disability, you know how difficult the road can be. Consider sharing your experience with another person with a similar challenge. Several organizations are currently supporting this effort (i.e., National Disability Mentoring Coalition) and would be grateful for your support.

6. Explore coaching and mentoring apps and platforms such as MentorPass, BetterUp, and The Muse to find out if their services are a good fit for you. Your mentor might not be geographically close, but that's the beauty of Zoom.

7. Check with your company to see if they have a mentoring program that you can participate in either as a mentee or a mentor. This is a great way to navigate the complexities of a career in the corporate world.

8. Minority groups have often felt like they lacked adequate resources and guidance. Join one of these groups to help even the playing field by helping with funding, getting on board seats, and leadership training.

9. Become a youth mentor at the local community center, Junior Achievement, or your church. Many organizations would welcome your heartfelt contribution.

10. Work with refugee families as they assimilate into a new world. They often need life skills, language, and job search training to become productive citizens within their new communities.

Notes:

Gratitude

How many times a week do you have moments where you feel like your efforts are completely underappreciated, whether you are dealing with surly teens, inattentive spouses, or frazzled co-workers? For many, this disappointment shows up routinely. Often enough, when we receive no thanks from others when we do something for them, we ask ourselves, "What's the point?" They don't seem to notice or care.

Gratitude and feeling valued are closely tied together, along with a pay-it-forward attitude. People who are seen and appreciated are more likely to help others in the future because they feel good about their actions. Further, gratitude is contagious. When I am in a receiving mode, I feel grateful for good things coming my way, large and small. I become more satisfied with my life, more resilient, and less affected by negative people and challenging circumstances.

Everyone is anxious these days. Between the daily barrage of bad news, concern about the market, interest rates, supply chain issues, inflation, job reductions, the safety of our children at school or shoppers at the mall, and global politics, we are all on high alert all the time. It can be hard to feel grateful when we are coming from a place of pain, fear, or anxiety. We know we will sleep better and feel more hopeful and less stressed if we can just close the door to our monkey mind, but it's not that easy to stop the chatter.

I work hard at shifting my focus to positive thoughts, and I actively seek to feel grateful for what is right in my life. Concentrating on what isn't working, what I don't have, or what others are doing or not doing is frustrating and upsetting. So, I head to yoga or the gym, pick up an inspirational book, or listen to a podcast about an exciting innovation. When I'm grateful for the small things, my overall mental health and well-being are significantly improved.

Gestures need not be grandiose to show another that they are valued. But, each time we do, we lift them up and fill our collective pool with just a little more kindness, which makes all of us feel better. You will be given many opportunities this week to show appreciation. What can you do to make gratitude a habit? Below are some ideas:

1. Include a gratitude affirmation in your email signature block. It's a way for recipients to learn about the things and values that are important to you.

2. Say thank you to underappreciated people (i.e., clerks, waiters, call centers). Include notes in tip jars along with the change. Put yourself in their shoes. What would make your day?

3. Help a favorite business or service provider succeed by giving them a shout-out online for their outstanding work or the great qualities of the products they provide.

4. Create a gratitude jar filled with appreciative notes for someone. They can read them daily or when they need a boost. Make one for yourself, too!

5. Creative? Go the extra mile and design personal thank you cards online using resources like Canva or Zazzle to say thank you to someone.

6. Be generous with your compliments to strangers. Tell someone who works hard in their yard that it is beautiful and that it makes you happy when you walk by. The effects of kindness can never be overestimated.

7. Call your mentor to show appreciation and let them know how their special qualities and advice have enhanced your life.

8. Let someone's manager know they are doing a great job, measurably contributing to the company, and are a wonderful asset. Make sure it is in writing with a copy to HR to be placed in their file—an important measure for annual salary evaluation.

9. Think about the charities that work diligently on issues that are important to you and consider a donation, volunteer your time, or post a comment on their website expressing why their work is so valuable and why it touches you.

10. How many times have you invited people for dinner or out to do something fun and it has never been reciprocated in any way or form? It can be discouraging and it takes the steam out of your efforts to grow the friendship. Have you unconsciously done the same thing? Be aware.

Notes:

Grief

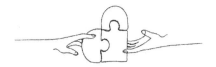

At some point, we have all experienced loss. Grief is our response to it, a process we go through to get to the other side. It looks different for each of us even though we are told there are well-mapped out stages to this feeling: shock, denial, anger, bargaining, depression, acceptance, and reflection.

Grief can be triggered by the loss of a loved one or the passing of a family pet. We experience it when our relationships change with others because of divorce, relocation, or a sense of growing apart. Unexpected job losses or a change in our financial security may cause us to feel like we have taken unwanted steps backward from a place we had arrived at through hard work.

The process is difficult and painful, and we may have trouble focusing, or we may experience forgetfulness, sometimes described as brain fog. Many become more irritable, less patient, and have zero tolerance for other people's problems, which can seem small in the face of their own. Others become isolated with little energy to do anything except feel the enormity of their loss, and some may lose themselves in a pint of their favorite ice cream to numb the pain.

Because the heartbreak of grief can increase blood pressure and the risk of blood clots, intense grief can alter the heart muscle so much that it causes "broken heart syndrome," a form of heart disease with the same symptoms as a heart attack.

The world is currently experiencing collective grief as we witness the loss of life due to warring factions and massive climate change catastrophes on the heels of a global pandemic that affected all of us. Each day, with global media access at our fingertips, we watch families trying to regain their footing in the face of insurmountable odds, and we ache for them, unsure of how to help.

Validating these feelings of sorrow and seeking out resources such as therapy, support groups, and self-care practices like meditation and exercise helps. Fortunately, there are groups such as GriefShare, HelpGuide, and HealGrief, to name just a few. These groups are often attached to places of worship and civic organizations or found on social platforms like Meetup. Help is abundant.

If someone you know is grieving, it can be hard to know what to say or do to help them. Here are some tips on how you can support them:

1. Help a loved one with funeral arrangements, sorting through personal effects, and the administrative details of closing the last chapter of a person's life—all of the things they hoped they would never have to face.

2. Honor the memory of a loved one who has passed by creating a memory book or planting a tree in their honor. Create a sense of connectedness and closure.

3. Gift a self-care basket to a friend going through a broken relationship that contains bath products, an inspirational journal, a gift certificate for a yoga class or massage, and a sleep mask.

4. Help a displaced family by opening your door to temporary housing and assist them in finding long-term housing, jobs, language skills, and emotional support groups.

5. Join a Care Committee at your place of worship or a service organization. Offer to help with practical things like cooking, cleaning, or running errands. Be invisible if that is what they

need while you give them the comfort of support.

6. Create beautiful note cards with personal photos and send them to friends who are feeling sad. Avoid offering clichés, commentary, or unsolicited advice.

7. Take a family a home-cooked meal. Hearty meals like casseroles, slow-cooker meals, soups, and stews are ideal comfort food for someone who is heartbroken.

8. Create a grief kit to support children and their caregivers in their grieving journey. It can contain books, activities, and resources to help in their healing process.

9. In addition to donating money to a charity meaningful to the bereaved, donate your time. Then, write a note explaining how the experience touched you and made you think of their loved one.

10. Create a treasure box of personalized messages, ones they can read each day for a specific period of thirty days up to a year to let them know you care.

Notes:

Home

Home means different things to each of us, but the one thing that remains consistent is it is a place we have an emotional connection to—a space that reflects who we are, our history, the things that interest us, and the community of people we care about. It's where we are most comfortable being our authentic selves with all of our quirks and flaws.

It can be a house, tent, apartment, or boat. It can be owned, rented, or borrowed. Over our lifetime, we will likely have many physical homes, each representing who we are and who we are becoming at that point in time. Some things will remain the same as we move from place to place with our personal items, family members, and pets. Other things such as size, style, colors, or location may change and reflect our current needs, dreams, desires, and the world around us.

Ultimately, though, home is not about the physical structure. It's an intangible that shows up as a feeling or a state of mind. With luck, it's a haven and a comfort zone, a sanctuary to live in peacefully, and it gives us a sense of security, control, identity, and privacy in a world that often feels frenetic and unexpected. For many, their deepest desires are to create homes that do not resemble the homes of their childhood, which do not hold positive memories. Their dream is to design a new vision and version of home.

We put a lot of effort into the structures we call our homes, but not everyone can afford to purchase a home, and, often, many feel "less than" renting. Most of the unhoused do not feel seen or acknowledged since our name and address are our principal identifiers. When home becomes strictly a physical structure rather than the attributes that represent it—a place where we feel safe and accepted—then we are left yearning.

What does home mean to you? Does it reflect your dreams and desires and the things that give you comfort? Beauty is in the eye of the beholder—is it beautiful to you? Can you help others create a sense of home and belonging that is perfect for them? Here are a few ideas, but I know you will find many more:

1. Create a space that reflects your true personality, with colors that bring you joy and peace. Fill it with special items that represent memories, art you have collected on your travels, hobbies, or collections that represent your interests.

2. Close off unused areas in your home from heat and air conditioning. Caulk and weatherstrip doors and windows. Use the money you save for a special decorating project.

3. Sign up for a team at Habitat for Humanity to help build a home for a deserving family.

4. Repair items and re-use envelopes, jars, paper bags, and scrap paper. Recycle when you can't. Purge items you seldom use and rent or borrow them when needed so your mind feels as clutter-free as your physical space.

5. Limit water usage each time you turn on the faucet. Consider contributing a well to a village to enhance the homes and lives of the locals.

6. Start an herb garden in your kitchen and bring the outside in with light and greenery. Enjoy the sensory aspects of your herbs when cooking.

7. Help a displaced family get settled by offering them your home

temporarily or providing items to help them create a new space that feels like home.

8. Designate a project space decorated in ways that inspire you to create and innovate, and write and dream.

9. Create a guest bedroom that feels like a sanctuary for those you invite in. Small considerations like flowers, books, candles, and a comfortable bed can make guests feel valued and appreciated.

10. Go for cozy and switch out fluorescent lighting to warmer shades of white and yellow. Then add additional lighting with well-placed lamps, strings of lights, or flameless candles. Lighting directly contributes to our mental health.

Notes:

Love

I've always said that life is a romantic business that is more inclusive than the romance experienced by two people in love. It's a view of life through a lens that gives us hope and a sense of anticipation, allowing our hearts to skip a beat when something feels magical, serendipitous, or "in the flow."

Living in love is shown through our actions and behavior toward other beings; it's how we interact with the world around us. Most of us experience love as a mix of human emotions like respect, affection, protectiveness, warmth, and appreciation toward our pets, friends, family, and nature each day. We are offered opportunities to be vulnerable in ways that may surprise, inspire, and motivate us. In each instance, we are taught empathy and humility, and we are given a chance to sacrifice for others and to compromise.

In contrast, *being in love* is generally limited to the one person who has connected exclusively with our heart on a deeper and more profound level. Love requires commitment and compassion for it to last from day to day. It can vary in intensity and change over time as relationships evolve or dissolve. We certainly see this in romantic relationships, which can be all-consuming in the initial stages, breathless and lusty. Later, they can evolve into relationships steeped in respect, patience, and a deep sense of knowing. Alternately, they may falter because they lack the depth to be self-sustaining and the parties leave disillusioned and disappointed.

You may have heard of the word "agape," which means selfless or unconditional love. It's the deepest form of love one can offer as it's given without expecting anything in return. Often more aspirational than attainable, most of us agree that the world would be a better place if we experienced this universal love more often.

Sometimes, we take those we love for granted, but this week is the perfect opportunity to be grateful to all sources of love and to expand and grow our definition. Here are some ideas you might consider:

1. Go on an adventure! Surprise someone and give them a break from the daily drudgery of a long list of "to-do" tasks. Purchase tickets to a game or concert, pack a picnic, or plan a weekend getaway.

2. Write a list of all of the reasons you love someone. You can be creative and use the first letters of their name to start each reason. Then, send it to them in a beautiful card.

3. Read *The Five Love Languages* by Gary Chapman with your partner and explore how you can better serve each other's needs.

4. Laughter is the music of the soul! Make someone laugh, watch a funny movie, or take them to a comedy club to lift their spirits.

5. Show physical intimacy. It can be as simple as meaningful eye contact, a comforting hand on the shoulder, or taking a friend's hand to let them know you are there for them. Actively try to keep the spark alive in a more intimate relationship.

6. Food is a way to the heart. Bring someone their favorite snack, prepare a candlelit dinner, or wake them with breakfast in bed.

7. Put the phone away. Don't scroll and talk, maintain eye contact, and be an active listener. Be interested and ask questions, including seeking out other's advice to show you value it.

8. Anticipate another person's needs, and thoughtfully do favors for them to lighten their load. Attach no conditions to these acts

of service. Think of them as random acts of kindness, not a tally.

9. Celebrate someone else's wins as if they were your own. Be their number one supporter and set aside any feelings of jealousy or wistfulness for your own success as you do the happy dance for them.

10. Make a habit of connecting. Say "I love you" in person, through little messages or occasional texts…but do so with abandon.

Notes:

Play

All work and no play makes Jill a boring girl and Jack a dull boy. Those of us who are prone to be workaholics have heard that admonishment from friends egging us on to join them for a fun time. Meanwhile, we stare resolutely at commitments and obligations. It's hard to let our hair down when we feel under the pressure of a long task list that never seems to get any shorter.

But, play is just as important for adults as it is for children! Stepping away from our work routines can keep us feeling engaged and energetic. There is no life-changing goal in sight when you play. The idea is to find joy without seeking a specific result outside of a good-natured competitive race to the end of the board or field with a friend. In other words, taking a bike ride because it's fun, not because the goal is to lose weight. Or playing Monopoly for the companionship, not growing your stash of plastic hotels.

Play takes on many forms. *Physical play* includes dancing, attending sports events, or going skiing with family and friends. *Social play* may include enjoying the company of girlfriends at a cooking class, sitting on the beach and watching the sunset with loved ones, or indulging in fantasy by dressing up as your favorite character.

Play improves our relationships in addition to contributing to health benefits like stress reduction and warding off depression. We all love someone who can make us laugh or smile. It's an endearing trait that breaks the ice and opens the door to new friendships and collaboration. More and

183

more companies are encouraging their employees to play and collaborate, with game stations to help foster team building, productivity, and goodwill.

This week, if you find you have a break in your afternoon, take a pause and remember that you don't need another person to play. You can amuse yourself with games that may have the additional benefit of preventing memory problems and improving brain function such as chess, puzzles, and lately, Wordle, while you try to best yesterday's score.

While play may seem frivolous, or even silly, we know it's important to our well-being, both physically and emotionally. Adults need recess, too! If you have forgotten how, then below are a few ideas to kickstart your week:

1. Summertime concerts in the park are a great way to let your hair down, enjoy being outside, listen to upbeat music, and have a picnic with family or friends.

2. Try "game-ifying" a task by adding points, rules, and some competition so that you get more into, and out of, the activity while making it fun. Each day, try and beat your old score.

3. Grab a journal and write down what your inner critic says every time you feel guilty about taking time to play. Then, underneath it, write whether it's true or a harsh imprint that does not serve you.

4. Join a pickup game of bocce ball, pickleball, or basketball with a neighbor or friend and take some time to enjoy the camaraderie.

5. If you enjoy building collections, go on a day trip and treat it like a scavenger hunt for items that you can add to your trove.

6. Imagine what would be a learning experience or fun for a small child and create a children's picture book complete with illustrations. Then share it with a small friend.

7. Learn how to create a charcuterie board and then invite some friends over to play board games and sample your creation.

8. If you enjoyed performing as a child for your parents, consider community theater as a creative way to have fun, either as a performer or supporter.

9. Give yourself a little love and plan a self-care night complete with a candlelit bubble bath, a rom-com, chocolate, and a cozy fire.

10. Think about your favorite childhood games and consider making bread or taking a pottery class as a substitute for Play-Doh, or an art class in lieu of fingerpainting.

Notes:

Humility

Why is it that we are attracted to humble people? Those rare and unique personalities are free from pride, arrogance, or an air of superiority. They are likable because they stand with us, feel reachable, and are not distanced.

Often money, power, and popularity change people in a way that puts other people off. They may have an elevated opinion of themselves and are convinced that they have created their own success with zero assistance—that no one else has, or can, add relevant value as they make their way down life's path.

In fact, many of us have had to march through life *seemingly* alone, street fighters in a world that moves at a different pace than ours. Because of a series of unfortunate circumstances, it may seem that the world has never been on our side and that any sliver of success is 100 percent our doing. And so, we talk incessantly about our victories, showing our strength, and remain continually on the defensive, believing we are under attack from others.

When your heart has been bruised, it's very easy to create a story as a tool to heal, but stories are often fiction. Fortunately, endings can be revised to happy, authentic ones. It starts by taking note of how you respond to people or situations. Do you believe you need to prove yourself daily through your words and actions? Or are you internally confident in your abilities? Do you welcome new information and offer assistance?

Do you feel isolated and alone or part of a community? How much energy do you spend seeking approval from people who are dismissive and negative rather than surrounding yourself with those who are positive and encouraging?

The only person we need to quietly convince is the (wo)man in the mirror because if we constantly praise ourselves to others, it can come off as arrogant and self-absorbed. And, it should never be substituted with false modesty, which is not humility. There is no place for falsely portraying helplessness, a lack of power, or self-deprecating humor.

Is there a way to achieve success and stay "low to the ground" (the very root of the word humility), and avoid getting caught up in a superficial life? Yes! By keeping our focus outward rather than inward and leaning toward giving, not getting. Since our practice of great-itude is stealth, this is a perfect week to remind yourself that you are unique and different but still a valuable piece to the *collective* whole. Below are some ways:

1. Practice anonymous humility by doing three to four secret and random acts of kindness this week. Only you will know the good you've done for someone.

2. Review your social media posts. Are you constantly posting selfies or posts seeking sympathy or approval, hoping for emojis that represent *likes*, *love*, or *care*?

3. Teach a young person to apologize to people by looking them in the eyes, making sure their words are genuine, and then supported by their actions.

4. Check in this week. Are you unconsciously living in the sunlight of others by name-dropping to gain importance because of who you know, not what you do?

5. Volunteer for the sake of it, not for bragging rights. Are you supporting a charitable organization because you want it to succeed, or are you only trying to make yourself look good?

6. Write unexpected thank-you notes this week to acknowledge the various people who made your success possible.

7. If you are part of a team, make a concentrated effort this week to give credit where it's due and highlight the team's success over your individual achievements.

8. Teach your children to ask for help and feedback when they need it. Part of being humble is recognizing our shortcomings and limitations and showing a willingness to learn from others.

9. Everyone has an opinion, and armchair quarterbacks are rarely appreciated. How many times can you silence your opinions this week to give voice to others?

10. Teach your children or grandchildren that their time is not worth more than anyone else's and they can show this by being on time or allowing others to go first.

Notes:

Inspiration

The word "motivation" is often mistakenly substituted for the word "inspiration." But, there is a difference between the two. Motivating another is prodding them to make money or achieve a result. It's task-oriented. Inspiration, on the other hand, is flaming the fire within to do better or to encourage someone to become an improved version of themselves. The focus is on internal qualities, not external results.

We all have people who inspire us, who fill us with enthusiasm and make us want to do more with our lives. When we are around them or read or hear about them, we feel energized and motivated to be the best we can be. We admire the lives they have led and the way they have overcome the obstacles they have faced. We admire the values they exhibit.

What are the special traits that draw us to these shining stars? For me, it's encouragement and possibility. I'm inspired to face difficult circumstances with compassion and to stand up for my personal values and beliefs. They model this for me as they advocate for those who are disadvantaged without shying away from challenges. They aim to make a difference in the world. They believe in themselves, admit their faults, and celebrate their wins. They take responsibility, and…they act.

The truth is that we often find we have many of the traits of the very people and things that inspire us—perhaps not in terms of their experiences but in values. We are drawn to them because we yearn to be perceived as like-minded. The good news is that you are! If you consider the reasons why you appreciate certain traits in another, you likely had an experience in your life that shifted your perception of the world and drew you to those with the same values. Like attracts like!

Most of us want to be inspirational to others, but something may be holding us back from showing the world all that we are. The difference between you and those who inspire you is that they show the world precisely who they are. It might seem like a tall order but here are some ways you can do the same:

1. Be enthusiastic and positive. Present yourself with high energy. Low energy shows up as boredom and disinterest. Passion and enthusiasm are contagious in the best kind of way.

2. Encourage your teens to be courageous. Suggest they give their first public speech, show up as their authentic selves, or stand up for their personal values. Then, check in!

3. Show someone that you care and are empathetic to their situation. Serve a meal at a shelter and say hello to someone who is homeless today. Ask how they are. Invisibility is hard.

4. Find something that you are passionate about and invest your time to learn more about it. Share your newfound knowledge as a speaker or in a continuing education workshop.

5. A little compliment can go a long way to boosting another's confidence and self-worth. Hand them out freely today.

6. Have coffee with a friend today who is struggling with a health or financial issue. Help them come up with a few strategies they can use to help alleviate the situation. Be positive and optimistic with a "Can Do" outlook.

7. Reach out to someone who is new at work, your club, or at your church by inviting them out to lunch with others from the group. Bring them into the fold by making them feel welcome and included.

8. Share your experience and speak at a job club to remind others that the right position is just around the corner. Give them actionable items to help them move forward successfully.

9. Entrepreneurship can be tough and lonely. Offer to do a brainstorming session with someone starting a new business and help them find solutions to some of the challenges they are facing.

10. Do you have an inspirational mantra that you live by? Share it with others as a tag in your email, on the back of your business card, in your voicemail greeting, or with personal handwritten notes to friends who could use a lift.

Notes:

Purpose

Having a purpose in life is one of the most fundamental human needs and, without it, we can feel lost or unsure of the next steps. It dictates how we choose to spend our days, whether our work is an avocation or a vocation, and who and how we love.

Our happiness quotient is directly tied to purpose. If we have a sense of purpose, we tend to be more positive, stepping into each day with joy and enthusiasm. It gives us a sense of motivation and direction, and it's a reason to get out of bed every morning. We believe that our lives matter and that we make a difference.

These days, purpose has renewed importance. Most of us in the post-pandemic world are more focused than ever on finding work that fills our emotional well-being as well as meeting our financial needs. We are looking for meaningful work that satisfies our desire to make a difference—but not if it comes at a loss to our families and not at the expense of our values and goals.

For many people, finding their purpose in life is not always obvious. Caught up in the day-to-day tasks of living, we may not take the time to address this hunger to have richer and more fulfilling lives. We often feel like we are treading water and not making any real progress toward our goals or our dreams—or even finding the time to clarify what they are.

Thinking about defining our purpose can be daunting to many, but we need to be clear that we have more than one purpose. Imagine how terrible we would feel if we thought we only had one and never found it! We have different purposes depending on the context of families or parenting, career, religion, activism, artistic pursuits, or contributions to the community.

You may have fulfilled one or two and are still trying to figure out the rest. If so, you are exactly where you are supposed to be. The Japanese word *ikigai* loosely translates to "your reason for getting up in the morning."It may change from day to day, and it might mean getting your children fed and to school on time one day or applying for a new job the next.

Below are a handful of ideas you may find helpful as you think about your purpose(s):

1. Take an inventory of what you have in your life and why it was important to you in the beginning when you acquired it. See if it still is today.

2. Think of a social cause that interests you or bothers you. Study and learn more about it so you can speak about it with certainty and back it up with facts.

3. Write out your story, your experiences, and the lessons you have learned. Purpose is nearly always connected to our values, and our values are a result of our life events.

4. Create a taste test or new adventures to try. Fill the calendar with things to look forward to—ones that may spark a sense of purpose.

5. Get involved with intergenerational programs. You may be a student searching for housing and willing to work part-time at a seniors' center. Or a senior looking to stay relevant in today's world through workshops and classes.

6. Feeling frustrated or annoyed in your role? Get specific and write down the things that bother you, then pick a couple of them and take action to better the situation.

7. Plan a trip to somewhere you have always wanted to go and

reflect on why you are drawn to this location. Are there commonalities with others on your travel list?

8. Volunteer with Meals on Wheels and deliver meals to the elderly or people with disabilities who could use a friendly face and a healthy meal. Ask them about their lives and the dreams that propelled them forward.

9. Sign up for weekly blogs and newsletters in the innovation space and read stories about social entrepreneurs who have created businesses with a social purpose.

10. Watch and be inspired by *Nobelity* and *One Peace at a Time*, documentaries offering insights by Noble Peace Prize winners and their path to purpose.

Notes:

Intuition

We all have an inner voice, the whisper in the night as we are falling asleep or the incessant one throughout the day arguing with our logical brain and demanding we act in a way that seems out of character, or even risky or nonsensical. Yet, the guidance we are given is often right—at least right for us—if we just listen and act.

Why are some people perceived as more intuitive than others, gifted with a sixth sense of knowing what lies ahead? Because they pay attention to their innermost thoughts instead of being driven by external pressures or a monkey mind chattering and reinforcing old patterns and behaviors. They are self-aware and pay attention to the way they feel physically and emotionally in every decision they make.

Intuition doesn't always show up as "light bulb" moments, giving us clarity or a great idea. It can be covert and manifest itself physically through sensations in our bodies such as a "pit" in our stomach, a tightness in our chest, restless sleep, or teeth grinding. If you are experiencing any of these symptoms and signals, it may be time to figure out what is weighing on you and put it to rest. Or perhaps it's the voice of inspiration knocking at the door to your heart with a great idea. It may be whispering, "Pick me. You can make a difference!"

By learning to trust and rely on our intuition, we can unlock a powerful means to help us navigate the complexities of life with greater ease and confidence. We often become better at reading non-verbal communication cues from others and will quickly understand what they are saying between the lines, which can help us identify potential roadblocks or obstacles in our relationships before they become major issues.

It takes a certain amount of courage to color outside of the lines and to rely on our inner wisdom, but the rewards can be immense. This week, if you notice a strong instinct to do something or move away from it, take a chance. Trust the message, see what develops, and then reflect on the outcome. We spend an inordinate amount of time trying to convince ourselves of a different answer when our heart says otherwise. Below are some ways that you can support your intuition this week:

1. Our intuition comes from aligning with our core values, and its purpose is to help us be true to ourselves. Place a list of your top ten core values where you can see them each day.

2. Flip a coin if you are struggling with an answer. As you release it, pay attention to the side you hope it will land on. Your internal voice is speaking to you.

3. Use evening meal prep as a time to quiet the mind. Do something repetitive such as chopping vegetables or kneading bread that requires little brain power and ask your intuitive mind for guidance on a problem or ideas for a project.

4. Check out *The Artist's Way* by Julia Cameron and start your day writing "morning papers," a free and uninhibited stream-of-consciousness writing time that can clear your mind for new ways to view situations.

5. Many apps and board games test your intuition, even the old Magic 8 Ball game. Practice while you play.

6. Buy yourself an art journal at your local art store and explore your feelings throughout the day. Draw, paint, doodle, collage, and sketch without too much intention or direction.

7. Go on a daily walking meditation and focus only on nature or

the sidewalk ahead of you, clearing space for new information to bubble up. Leave all technology behind and practice repeating your favorite mantra.

8. You might find it interesting to explore what's behind your dreams if you are an active dreamer. Spend time at your local library researching many interesting studies.

9. Get in tune with your body and explore yoga to learn to scan it and be fully present with where it is each day and why.

10. Are those things that seem magical really serendipity? Or, did you set them in motion unconsciously by your actions? Follow your enthusiasm, be aware, and find meaning in the unexpected. Create your own luck.

Notes:

Reliability

None of us wants to associate with companies or individuals that we can't depend on, and we don't want to buy products that we've learned break easily. Although we use the words interchangeably, "reliability" is generally associated with *things* whereas "dependability" is about *people*. In other words, the outcomes of science experiments should be reliable, and we expect our partners to be dependable. Both words ultimately create trust.

Personally, I equate reliability with safety—the safety of eating at my favorite neighborhood restaurant, buying a particular brand of sports equipment, boarding a plane while believing it's been well maintained, or staying at a certain hotel chain focused on stellar guest service. Reliability is of paramount importance for businesses. It underpins their reputation and keeps their customers coming back and referring others to their products and services.

It's a foundational pillar and core value of most organizations, and its reach extends to the employees. When they are conscientious and treat everyone with respect and empathy, they are viewed as trustworthy by the business and are offered more opportunities to be involved in important projects. Being dependable is a hallmark of personal success, and their success is critical to the company's well-being.

In our personal lives, knowing that we can call on someone who will be there and who has our back is a great comfort to most. Their actions show they value and appreciate us, our time, and our interests. As always, we get what we give. If we show up late because we have forgotten an appointment or are overcommitted, we make others feel less valued and can be viewed as self-absorbed and unreliable. Dependability is a cornerstone of good friendships.

I avoid unwelcome surprises by having people that I can trust as part of my circle, and I find that I level up my own game because they expect the same from me. It's always good to check in. Look at your dependability quotient this week and that of your support network. Below are some ways:

1. Write a list of friends and co-workers who are consistently there for you with a description of how that shows up. Then make a list of friends and coworkers who depend on you and the ways you come through for them.

2. Reflect on the people you consider to be "energy suckers" in your life and why you continue to engage with them. Consider ways you can minimize contact.

3. Review your social media accounts and make sure your personal brand is reflected accurately (i.e., the things people say about you when you leave the room). Use examples, not just words. Does it reflect dependability through actions?

4. Go through your emails and messages and confirm that you have responded to everyone who contacted you to either continue the conversation or close it.

5. Give your children or grandchildren chores at home and reward them for their completion, thoroughness, and regularity. Dependability is a quality that grows with appreciation.

6. Practice saying "No" if you feel overcommitted. It's honest and will continue to show you are trustworthy.

7. Take a dance class with your partner and learn to trust their lead. Step away from gender-specific roles and take turns

practicing leading the other.

8. Join a handful of teams. Volunteer with a local charity, play league sports, or join a board. Practice fulfilling your role and being a valued and dependable asset.

9. Coach a young person's athletic team, teaching them the meaning of dependability, loyalty, and consistency.

10. Take a leadership workshop with a young professional and then meet weekly to discuss ways to show dependability and accountability at work as well as at home.

Notes:

Magic

I have always been a dreamer in search of a magical life, one of wonder and awe. It allows me to believe in possibilities, and it gives me comfort that I have "behind the scenes" support if I am open to experiences outside of the boundaries that I have placed upon myself.

I'm in good company with other hopefuls. The original explorers who traveled the world looked for the unexplored, mysterious, and untouched as they imagined rewards and the freedom to create in newfound places. Scientists searching for vaccines and cures do so pragmatically but with an inkling of hope that miracles just might exist. Our young people, untainted by daily challenges, dream of their prince or princess and of finding treasure at the beach.

Seeing the world through the eyes of a child always feels magical to me. My five-year-old grandson is thrilled when he breaks a rock open and finds crystals, puts cookies out for Santa on Christmas Eve while dreaming of the morning stash to come, or leaves his special gift of a tooth for an imaginary fairy, hoping she will see the value in one of the few personal gifts he has to offer. I revel in his sense of awe, happy to be away from the world of practicality and black-and-white answers.

We cannot force magic to happen, but we can help it unfold in our lives just by keeping our eyes wide open to the smallest indications of its presence and then…believing! If you are worried about finances, do you pick up the penny on the pavement and say thank you, believing it's a sign that more is on the way? Or, do you walk by it with barely a glance because of its insignificance against the amount you believe you need? Magic and faith go hand in hand, and watching for signs of it is the first step.

Living a magical life is an art. It is a way of looking at things, a way to help you bring light into your life. So, how will you find that little bit of magic today that puts a spring in your step and a sparkle in your eyes? Magic is in the smallest of details, so stay vigilant. Below are some ideas:

1. Live in a space of wonder. Ask at least one question a day that seems nonsensical and fun like "What would the world be like if pigs really could fly?"

2. Reverse engineer everything to understand how you are connected to everyone and everything around you. Six degrees might just be three!

3. Go on a walk with a small child. Study the beauty of the forest, the ocean, a plant, or the stars, and explain your relationship to it.

4. Play on the edge. Do something you have never done before that might seem frightening: give a speech, sing at karaoke night, or go on a trip alone. Marvel at your courage!

5. Enrich your life by giving something precious to another—your time, a gift of something they have admired, or an experience——and feel their gratitude.

6. Surprise a stranger with a random act of kindness. Feel the mysterious joy of knowing that they have no idea where this unsolicited and anonymous gift came from.

7. Take a friend to the planetarium or a 3D nature show at IMAX that will leave you in awe of nature's synchronicity.

8. Share your *big* dreams and encourage others to do the same! See if you can help someone else's dream come true. It will create a

magical experience for you both!

9. Invite someone special to an art class and create with abandon together.

10. Go on a volunteer trip and make a difference in another person's life. A full heart is one filled with magic.

Notes:

Nurturing

Most relationships need nurturing, that extra time and attention you invest to help an individual grow or to make your connection stronger. We often associate the word "nurturing" with children, but it applies equally to marriage, client development, or spending quality time with a new employee that needs cultivating.

We show this caring quality when we pet our fur babies or water and tend to our plants. We care about them and want them to thrive. And, we know all children need encouragement to develop into their best selves. It takes a willingness on our part to understand how best we can help them, which may include other compassionate resources in addition to our own.

The phrase *it takes a village to raise a child* is from an African proverb, a reminder that it takes many people to create a healthy environment for children to flourish. The villagers can be neighbors, teachers, relatives, or friends who make themselves available to provide direct care or to support the parents in ensuring the welfare of every child. People with this gift are the ones others can count on when they need encouragement and attention.

We all need love, support, and nourishment but, sometimes, we forget to think about ourselves. Do you take time to stop, have a healthy meal, and get adequate sleep? Do you feed your brain with innovative ideas while learning new lessons? Do you "stop to smell the roses" and appreciate all that is yours? We often put ourselves last, but we are the best friend we have, and we don't want to lose sight of our own needs to be cared for.

This idea of a "village" may seem elusive with the morphing of the traditional family unit, career choices that often necessitate moving away from family to new locations, the increased cost of living that requires both parents to work to make ends meet with little time left to socialize, and increased isolation from company connections due to remote work. Even with these barriers, there are ways to reconnect, to show you care, and let others know you need support.

Once you start looking around, you'll find many opportunities to nurture both yourself and others. These activities don't take a lot of time—just a lot of heart:

1. Volunteer with an equine-assisted therapy organization dedicated to improving the physical, cognitive, and social well-being of children (and adults).

2. Read to preschoolers at your local daycare center or kindergarten in a disadvantaged neighborhood. For many, this may be a rare opportunity to have a story read to them and a gateway to a lifetime of reading and writing.

3. Stay connected and follow up regularly with your clients and business connections, adding value to their days without asking anything from them. Show you are there for them by your actions.

4. Help educate children on how to react during an emergency. Do you have a family emergency plan and emergency kit? Do they know how to call 911? Helping a child feel safe in all situations is a major component of nurturing.

5. Volunteer at a local food kitchen and help ensure that no one starts their day with an empty stomach. Consider starting a community garden in your neighborhood.

6. Visit a local homeless shelter and volunteer to spend a few hours playing with and bringing joy and a sense of normalcy to family members in the middle of a family crisis.

7. Volunteer at a children's hospital. Give a child a sense of self-worth by listening and validating their feelings at a time when they have lost any fragment of control they believe they have.

8. Nurture the creative spark inside by fanning the flames of an idea you have long thought about but have been afraid to share.

9. Monitor the online activity of your youth to protect them and their innocent view of the world.

10. Nurture yourself today. Be kind and give yourself some grace. What would you say to your younger self now that you are a grown adult?

Notes:

Patience

Our patience is continuously being eroded by the fast-paced, online, all-the-time world we live in. Face it—we want fast results whether it's a web search, a medical diagnosis, or a cure for an illness ravaging our world. This urge for instant gratification can lead to anger, frustration, poor judgment, irrational decisions, stress, and a negative attitude toward others.

Our tolerance is tested each time we are unwilling to wait for others or when they do things in a way we might not agree with. Even the people who are closest to us can frustrate us multiple times a day with their words and actions. And, it works both ways. Other people can become impatient with us, rolling their eyes, huffing, sighing, or tapping their feet. They can make us feel uncomfortable or angry.

Patience is a mark of respect, requiring us to take the time to pay attention to the other person's needs and words, which results in stronger, more considerate, relationships. This skill gives us the resources to tolerate serious setbacks in life such as an accident that requires long-term physical therapy or financial losses that impact our daily living. It helps us make more rational and realistic decisions that result in long-term impact, not just immediate satisfaction.

We may not be in control of the environment that we find ourselves in, but we can control how we choose to respond. Life is full of hassles. It can be tough to stay calm in traffic jams and deal with car troubles or broken computers. Here are some ways you can practice patience thoughtfully this coming week and maybe help others cultivate patience, too.

1. Be present and listen carefully to another person's opinion instead of thinking about how you're going to respond. You might learn something in addition to their respect.

2. Offer to let someone go ahead of you in the queue if they have a couple of items or are late making their connection flight when debarking. Remember how grateful you were when someone accommodated you.

3. Caught up in a new Netflix series? Practice patience and stop after one episode rather than binge-watching every episode in one sitting.

4. Tolerate the mistakes of others by offering help instead of criticism. Remember how you feel when you are judged. Each evening, write about your efforts to show grace in your journal.

5. Practice breathing techniques and take a sip of water to keep your blood pressure stable, fidgeting, squirming, finger tapping, feet jiggling, or other nervous gestures. Be actively conscious of your physical manifestations of impatience.

6. Play games and sports with your children. Do not make it a practice of letting them win just so they can feel good. Rather, teach them patience by allowing them to excel and let them enjoy the gratification that they won "fair and square."

7. Spend the morning focused on completing one task rather than multitasking, which kills focus and productivity and leads to a lack of quality. Often, anxiety levels rise when people divide their attention and don't have a continued sense of completion.

8. Have lunch with friends or prepare a nice dinner for your family. Relish each bite and the company that surrounds you rather than simply filling your belly. This is particularly

important if you are single and lack the social aspects of mealtimes.

9. Lend a helping hand to your kids or grandkids when you see chaos rather than complaining. You may not have created the mess, but it just might be you who turns the situation around.

10. Diversion is a great tactic when you are at the end of your rope. Step away from a trying situation and go for a run or a walk. Write the email but stash it away in your draft folder for 24-48 hours. Give a toddler a different toy or point out something super cool and interesting to avoid a meltdown.

Notes:

Poverty

Historically, poverty has been defined based on income and the ability to meet basic standards of living. The World Bank sets the international poverty standard at $1.90 per day. Anything below that is considered extreme poverty. Most of us cannot imagine trying to have our basic needs met on $60 per month: food, safe drinking water, clothing, sanitation facilities, health, shelter, education, etc.

Sadly, millions of people live in poverty. World poverty was on a steady decrease, but it's estimated that because of the COVID-19 pandemic and subsequent global recession, poverty rates have increased for the first time since 1990. Job losses, increased pressures of care and domestic work, reduced hours, and strains on both physical and mental health have impacted individuals and businesses, particularly women.

It's closer to home and to each of us—closer than you might think. All of us have witnessed poverty when we see the homeless walking the streets, but what many of us are not privy to are the empty refrigerators and lack of care in the poorer sections of our communities. Many children go to school each day hungry. Their families rely on services offered by nonprofits, government organizations, religious institutions, and people like you and me.

Poverty has many tentacles, including feelings of shame, powerlessness, hopelessness, and humiliation. It's a child lost to a preventable disease because of insufficient funds to pay a doctor. It's attending school in clothes that don't fit, and being on the outside looking in. It's a family living in a car or a shelter, vulnerable and exposed. The emotional scars are as devastating as the physical imprint.

Because we often think of poverty in terms of financial destitution, our first reaction is to give money. But, a handout is not the same thing as a hand-up. Tackling poverty means helping people to become educated and achieve jobs and healthcare. There are many ways that you can participate in the resolution of this issue. Here are some examples:

1. Reach out to a local school's administration office and offer your time and help by cleaning up, tutoring, supporting ongoing projects, or fundraising.

2. Research organizations (i.e. Charity:Water; WaterAid; Splash) that are making a difference in global water issues and find out how you can get involved. Twenty-six percent of the world's population doesn't have access to safe drinking water and 46 percent of the world's population has no access to basic sanitation needs.

3. Clean out your closets and take gently used items to charitable organizations like Dress for Success or Goodwill. Consider organizing a winter coat drive for the homeless.

4. Brighten the lives of children at Christmas who may have no expectation of Santa stopping by their house or shelter by organizing a toy drive or adopting a family.

5. Consider investing in microloans to help women in impoverished nations grow small businesses (see Kiva, AccionInternational, or Grameen America.) There are many books, films, and resources available to learn more.

6. Deliver meals to seniors in your local community through Meals on Wheels and provide social interaction to the homebound or isolated.

7. Put dollars directly into teacher's hands who are serving low-income students. Check out DonorsChoose to help fund supplies, field trips, and more.

8. Sort food, check expiration dates, and pack food for distribution at your local food bank. Create a team work event or bring together neighbors and friends to volunteer followed by pizza night at your favorite local spot.

9. Homelessness increased by twelve percent in 2023. Find ways to be part of the solution. Learn more through organizations like Invisible People Foundation, The Night Ministry, Operation Impact, The Right to Shower, and many more.

10. Many local organizations host backpack-filling events across the country before the school year. Come together as a family and set a child up for success by providing them with the tools they need to feel confident and on an equal footing with the other students in their class.

Notes:

Spontaneity

We are creatures of habit. Have you ever been to a workshop or conference and returned to the same seat at the end of each break feeling like you have a claim on it, that it's "your" seat? Do you sit in the same church pew every Sunday, drive the same route to the office, or eat the same daily breakfast?

There is a comfort to routine, but there is also a certain monotony attached to it as well. How many times in the past few weeks have you trusted your gut instinct, listening to the little voice inside rather than closing the door on it and opting for a comfort zone of familiarity?

If coming up with examples is a stretch for you, ask your friends and family about your routines. What may not be obvious to you often is to them. Some routines are good. Having habits like exercise, regular self-care, and meditating or praying can keep us productive and comfortable, but leaving free time to change things up can refresh your perspective on life.

There is something a little heady and naughty about being spontaneous when you have been raised in the structured environments of families, schools, and companies. It feels liberating to throw off the invisible chains and jump into a new experience. It helps you develop a "go with the flow" attitude from which you can become more flexible in other areas of your life.

We are often told that we should live in the present because the past is behind us and the future has yet to arrive and is uncertain. Trying to be prepared is understandable. But, if we free ourselves from constant planning and structure and take the "No" out of our vocabulary, we open our world up to unrehearsed possibilities. This ability to adapt to the unexpected helps us to avoid conflict and confrontation when things don't go according to plan.

Still feeling too antsy to throw caution to the wind? Take a minute and ask yourself this: What is the worst thing that can happen if you act on an impulse? Chances are good that when you really study it, there is very little risk. Here are some fun possibilities:

1. Keep track of your time for one week to see how much of it is filled with routine or unnecessary tasks and how much of your day is overbooked. Replace some of that time with activities that will expand your knowledge and inspire you.

2. Go out with a friend and change your appearance. Wear a wig, buy a fake nose ring, or apply a temporary tattoo. Create a role to match the new look.

3. Make a list of the seemingly impulsive things you have talked yourself out of using your head instead of your heart and whether you felt you regretted it later. In hindsight, were your concerns valid?

4. We routinely make online meal reservations but try meeting up in a fun part of town and randomly choosing a restaurant instead of planning ahead. Are you open to giving an unknown establishment a chance?

5. If you work remotely, change your office environment at least once a week from home to a coffee shop or the library for a change of atmosphere. Which is best for you and why?

6. Write a message, seal it in a glass bottle, and throw it in the ocean. If they can do it in a movie, why can't we? Share anything you would like the universe to know.

7. Engage in a meaningful conversation with one new person every day. Find out something interesting about them and then follow up with an email or coffee date.

8. Take a walk in the rain with a friend. Be a kid again—wear your sneakers, get messy, and jump in large puddles.

9. Make a list of five things that you have always been curious about, do a bit of research, and then give yourself a day off from chores to plan a trip or adventure around them.

10. Enjoy "Reverse Day" with your kids or grandchildren, a day full of laughter and brain twisters. Eat your dessert before dinner, read books from back to front, wear your clothes inside out, or call each other by your new names spelled backward.

Notes:

Resilience

We are all hard-wired to recover after failure, but how we adapt to adversity or hardship is an indicator of the level of resilience we have. This process of "bouncing back" from life-changing situations and stressful conditions is never-ending. It requires time and effort and, often, baby steps as we navigate grief and disappointment.

It takes resilience to survive, and we weren't born with it. Rather, we learn how to be resilient both functionally and emotionally on our life path. It shows up differently for each of us and is the product of several intersecting elements, including genetics, trauma, and personal development. What some may consider trying and difficult, others may find easy. This is not an indication that your resilience quotient is low, but rather that theirs has been buffered through certain challenges and yours through others.

The one thing that appears consistent is that a resilient attitude is generally an optimistic one. How many times have we heard that failure is not falling but staying down? We may pull ourselves back up, wobbly and confused, with less inflated expectations. We may be forced to adopt new views. But, each teaching moment increases our resilience and turns stressful situations into ones of understanding.

If we can come to terms with the fact that life is a journey, not a destination, it can provide new coping skills every day. Then we may find ourselves more capable of taking things in stride and honing our skill of resilience. If our life path has a sense of purpose and we surround ourselves with positive and supportive relationships, our ability to be resilient will grow in a healthy and powerful way.

Look at your level of resilience this week—the areas that feel strong and the others that need a little help. Here are some ideas that might help you or a friend:

1. Write down five obstacles you have faced in the past and how you overcame them. Then, next to each, add the lesson you learned from that experience.

2. Let children solve their problems. Don't be a helicopter parent! When parents are controlling, children have a harder time making personal decisions later in life. Instead, teach them that problem-solving can be fun.

3. Having a hard day? Practice self-compassion and self-acceptance! Do something nice for yourself. Tomorrow is a new day full of surprises and do-overs.

4. Take a class or workshop to enhance your critical thinking skills. Consider mediation training to help you listen to, and study, both sides of a conflict or argument as you help others resolve their differences or better understand your own position.

5. Create a vision board to clarify the direction you want your life to take and how you will get there. As you cut and paste, reflect on past challenges and the steps you took to overcome them, the support you received, and how faith in yourself moved you forward.

6. Feeling overwhelmed with the many tasks on your to-do list? Each night, leave a note to yourself by the coffeepot of just three achievable things you will accomplish the next day. One step at a time!

7. Adopt a 365-degree bird's eye view of each issue. Practice detachment. Imagine you are on a plane looking down at the

world, the situation, and the people in it. Gain perspective and journal about this experience. Revisit your entry in a couple of months.

8. Resilience works because of the support we both get and give. Seek it when you need it, and then return it this week to the friends and family who could use your helping hand and emotional support.

9. Storytelling can serve as a powerful and inspirational tool for others during tough times. Share your story over coffee, in a keynote or book, or with a teen who is lost and confused. Gather up friends and watch a documentary or movie about someone who overcame a daunting problem and thrived.

10. Foster a growth mindset and remind yourself and others that your goal is to build resilience, not just find Band-Aid resolutions. Resilience will teach you to pivot and adapt with greater ease when the next set of challenges arise—and they always do.

Notes:

Afterword

"The universe operates through dynamic exchange—giving and receiving are different aspects of the flow of energy in the universe. And in our willingness to give that which we seek, we keep the abundance of the universe circulating in our lives." ~Deepak Chopra

A global pandemic deepened the loneliness epidemic in America, but it was firmly rooted and rampant long before we were asked to isolate ourselves from other human beings. People have always yearned for the company of others and true friendship, not "likes" on social media posts or situational and momentary friends from monthly networking groups, religious gatherings, or quick workplace conversations at the communal coffee pot or on a video chat. Rather, the mythical ride-and-die friendships of Thelma and Louise or Butch and Sundance.

Concerned with rising suicide rates and other mental health challenges facing citizens, the U.S. Surgeon General issued a General Advisory calling attention to the fact that more than half of all Americans are lonely. He named it a top public health crisis: loneliness, isolation, and lack of connection. The reported effects are staggering. The mortality impact of being socially disconnected is equal to smoking up to 15 cigarettes a day, and even greater than those associated with obesity and physical inactivity.

Well over 100 countries have issued reports on loneliness in their countries and the impacts on their citizens. The statistics vary but not by much. Sixty percent of young people aged 18-22 say they are lonely, and those numbers are increasing at a rate outpacing that of their elderly counterparts. Over 30 percent of the global population has only two close friends, and 12 percent have none at all. Most are researching ways to address this disturbing trend.

Responding to the statistics that revealed that 700,000 Londoners feel lonely most or all the time, the mayor is building a strategy for social inclusion. The UK government has followed up on its commitment with about £30 million to increase volunteering opportunities, as well as substantial new investments in public awareness campaigns and research to better address loneliness. Heavily populated Brazil, Turkey, and India, the top three on the global loneliness scale, remind us that you can be surrounded by masses of people and still be lonely.

Is there a connection between loneliness and rising suicide rates? The CDC showed a record-high number of suicides in 2022, and they are increasing the fastest among people of color, younger people, and those who live in rural areas. Sadly, these numbers may be higher as suicides may be misclassified as drug overdoses, even if they were intentional. We know that rising financial stressors and longstanding difficulty accessing needed mental health care can be predictors of suicide, but we are now more aware than ever that loneliness is right up there with them.

Suicide and depression don't confine themselves to groups that might seem obvious to us. Living alone is a risk marker for suicide closely associated with adults with the highest levels of income and education, those with goals and plans to succeed who find themselves alone with no one to share their success or abundance with, or, quite frankly, their continued value, whether unemployed or retired. Many countries, including Sweden, are building intergenerational apartments as one avenue to address this issue.

Though I've never contemplated suicide, I have come face to face with loneliness and questioned my continued value to my family and the workforce. For many of us, and certainly in the world of business, our personal value has been attached to the financial rungs we climb and the job titles that are marks of success that we have earned. Our income supports our families, provides educational opportunities, and allows us to have outside interests and new experiences. As our children launch and the workforce attracts new blood, we often experience a sense of slippage much akin to the feeling of despair in a job loss.

Solutionaries—You are the Answer!, my first book, was written because others looking for purpose-driven work needed it. I wrote this book because I needed it to remind myself that each of us can be valued in many important ways and that we each bring an important and unique piece to the universal jigsaw puzzle. But, that also means *doing it*—even if we are adding value in a way that doesn't seem as apparent as the avenues of the past.

Often when we add spontaneous intentional change on top of uninvited change, it's easy to lose our bearings and question where we belong, how we can help fix the brokenness, and what value we bring to the equation. If we quit a job that wasn't right for us, we are faced with looking for a new source of income. If we move, we need to create a new support base. If we are returning to a school environment after a period of isolation, the myth we may have held about school may have evaporated. And, it can be lonely!

The immediate danger to our health and well-being from the silent beast that is COVID-19 has subsided, and we have been left to clean up the torched path it left behind. Many of us have opted not to return to the old normal, and we find ourselves in search of the Holy Grail—the desire to have lives that are as emotionally fulfilling as financially. We want time— time to be with loved ones, time to see the world, time to learn new skills, and time to experience richer lives. But, we can't do it alone, nor do we want to. We were born to be part of humanity, not bystanders watching from the perimeter.

We must be willing to give what we seek. It's a process called dynamic exchange—sometimes more simply known as the law of giving and receiving. If you want more, you must give more. Value is in the exchange with the universe, with others, and with our internal self. And, it's a gift offered in grace, without conditions or expectations, given purely and simply. Let's start there, just plant the seeds, and watch your bounty and your life expand and grow.

About the Author

Linda Lattimore is a dedicated, passionate collaborator and visionary. She is a well-regarded speaker and educator in the field of Sustainable Leadership. A seasoned lawyer, C-suite executive, business consultant/strategist, and board member, Linda supports and advocates for business models that consider the significance of positive corporate impact to stakeholders and the environment.

An American raised in Peru and Mexico, she has traveled extensively throughout the world and has witnessed firsthand some of the world's most pressing social issues. Linda is the Founder and Executive Director of the WGN Global Fund, a 501c(3) that joins forces with women in developing nations who, because of socioeconomic circumstances, would not otherwise have access to the education or funding opportunities needed to create small businesses.

Linda is committed to helping individuals, from our youngest generations to Boomers, understand the importance of their unique gifts and talents in a world in need. In 2018, she released *Solutionaries—You Are the Answer!* which became an immediate best seller. Today, she offers workshops to individuals searching for meaningful work and changemakers with innovative solutions, eager to launch their ideas and make a difference in our communities.

Linda enjoys digging in the dirt at the community garden close to her home in San Diego, sharing her bounty with home-cooked meals for friends, and throwing paint on the canvas that resides in her office as a dose of inspiration in between calls. But, the highlight of each day is the laughter of five small grandchildren under the age of eight who remind her daily that the best is yet to come.

Visit her site at **https://www.lindalattimore.com**.

Also by the Author

So.lu.tion.ary
[suh-**loosh**-*uh*-ner-ee]
noun

1. Disruptive innovator who creates transformational impact

2. Critical thinker who treats the root cause, not just the symptoms

3. Leader supporting a culture of innovation

4. Visionary who challenges conventional wisdom for a better way

Are you someone who hungers to make a difference in the world, but who doesn't know how?

Perhaps you are a Baby Boomer wishing you could leave a legacy or a young professional unsure about your skills and talents or where you want to work but certain that it needs to be with conscious companies. *Solutionaries* sets you on the right path by taking you through a process whereby you:

- Discover the talents, gifts, and tools that make you uniquely qualified to lead.
- Present your distinct value proposition to the world with intention.

- Identify compelling issues that drive you to serve and make a difference.
- Find and join your tribe of like-minded "Solutionaries" and changemakers.
- Create an action plan for a life that meets both your financial and emotional needs.
- And more!

For fans of:

- Zoe Weil's *The World Becomes What We Teach*
- Anthony Boquet's *The Bloodline of Wisdom*
- William MacAskill's *Doing Good Better*
- Leslie R. Crutchfield's *Do More Than Give*
- Peter Singer's *The Life You Can Save*

Buy link:
https://www.amazon.com/dp/1945847018

Made in the USA
Columbia, SC
13 February 2024

31434627R00130